*"In telling the real-life ... adversity and challenge because they had the passion, determination and sheer grit to succeed, Bill Ellis provides a handbook of inspiration for us all. This is a book to treasure, learn from and pass on to anyone you know is trying to win."*
**–Ingrid Vanderveldt, Founder and CEO - EBW2020**

*"I have been a huge fan of Bill's Friday's Fearless Brand series since its inception and consider every new article a must-read. Bill has an amazing knack for tapping into the mind and soul of each individual and sharing exactly what 'it' is that made them the fearless brands and successful people they became. His powerful insights are always relevant and provide his readers with wisdom that we can utilize in order to create our own fearless brands.* Women Who Won *does a remarkable job of capturing the spirit, drive and hearts of these high-achieving fearless brands. This book is certain to deliver inspiration, motivation and education to all readers, regardless of gender. Highly recommended!"*
**–Bob Burg, coauthor of *The Go-Giver***

*"Inspired! This book is a gift to our daughters (and our sons). It reminds us who we are and what we are capable of. These are 'portraits of possibility.' Thank you, Bill, for capturing these stories and telling them beautifully."*
**–Dondi Scumaci, Author of *Designed for Success,***
**_Ready, Set...Grow_ and _Career Moves_**

"Written out of respect for a tireless mother, awe of twin granddaughters, and an earnest desire to help all people see the beauty in a well-executed, communicated, and lived brand, Bill Ellis shares stories of women from around the globe who have inspired him and his countless followers on his Fearless Friday blog series. These stories will serve to inspire you to live a fuller life while embracing and honing your brand. This book is perfect for the entrepreneur, social entrepreneur, and any other seeking motivation, inspiration, and tangible tools for your own success."

**–Dafna Michaelson Jenet,**
**Founder of the Journey Institute, International**
**Best-selling author and Colorado State Representative**

"For years I loved reading Bill Ellis's Friday 'Fearless Brands' blog posts and secretly wished he'd compile his best into a book. Good news for all of us: he did! Bill's two-dozen-plus profiles of amazing women are poignant and powerful—but more than that, they are powerfully instructive. If you seek to build a clear-voiced, stand-out brand in this cluttered world (and who doesn't?), Women Who Won will be your road map, packed with inspiring insights you can model and use to win yourself!"

**–John David Mann, coauthor of the**
**national bestseller *The Go-Giver***

*"In his book,* Women Who Won, *Bill Ellis takes us on an impactful journey exploring the passion and purpose of women and their accomplishments. Through their stories of triumph, consideration, learning, and love, Ellis shows us what it means to stand in the unique values that defines each of us as individuals. Then, when those values are communicated clearly and confidently to others, we see the power of personal branding and legacy in how we can live life to the fullest and inspire others to do the same."*

**–Lida Citroën, International Personal Branding and Reputation Management Specialist, CEO, LIDA360, LLC**

*"One of the tenets of my life's philosophy is that 'One person attracted to you because of who you are can change your life forever.' In his book,* Women Who Won, *Bill Ellis presents 28 women who have changed lives because of who they have become. This collection of stories about amazing women accomplishing incredible things will change your life for the better. This is a must read."*

**–Dr. Tom Hill – Co-author of *Chicken Soup for the Entrepreneurial Soul, Blessed Beyond Measure* and *Living at the Summit***

# WOMEN
# WHO WON

## Stories of Courage, Confidence, Vision and Determination

### BILL ELLIS

**BIG** BILL'S BOOKS

# Women Who Won
*Stories of Courage, Confidence, Vision and Determination*
Bill Ellis

**BIG BILL'S** BOOKS

Published by Big Bill's Books, St. Louis, MO
Copyright ©2017 Bill Ellis
All rights reserved.

Editor: Tara Rogers-Ellis

Book design: Davis Creative, www.DavisCreative.com

**Library of Congress Cataloging-in-Publication Data**

Library of Congress Control Number: 2017907362

Bill Ellis

Women Who Won: Stories of Courage, Confidence, Vision and Determination

ISBN: 9780998757001

Library of Congress subject headings:

1. BIO022000 (Biography and Autobiography/Women)

2. BUS109000 (Business and Economics / Women in Business)

3. SEL021000 (Self-help / Motivational & Inspirational)

2017

*For the incredible women*
*who have so greatly and directly*
*enriched my life —*
*Billie, Abigail, Audrey and Tara*

# Table of Contents

*"I see women
the world over
as smart, gifted and
strong—with the talent
and commitment
to transform lives."*

**–Zaha Hadid**

# Introduction

## Winning Matters

*"We keep score in life because it matters.*
**Pat Summitt**

Is winning important? Pat Summitt certainly thought so.

Pat Summitt was one of the greatest coaches in basketball history. Her legacy of 1,098 victories still stands today as the NCAA record for most wins by any coach—male or female. In her 38 years as head coach at the University of Tennessee, she won eight national championships without having a single losing season. In fact, there were only two seasons when her Lady Vols' team won fewer than 20 games—and those were her first two seasons as coach.

Pat Summitt knows all about winning. She knows that winning is the result of hard work, determination, and fighting through every roadblock on the path. She knows that winning requires character.

Her path to success was filled with obstacles. At an early age, Summitt knew that she loved basketball, but there was no girls team at her high school. There were no university scholarships for women. She suffered a traumatic knee injury and was told she'd never play again.

But she didn't quit. As she put it, "Too many people opt out and never discover their own abilities because they fear failure. They don't understand commitment."

Those who seek to win often encounter obstacles that are neither anticipated nor fair. Winning is about making the effort and persisting in that effort, in spite of life's hurdles. Failure, on the other hand, is not even trying.

Strictly speaking, to win means to defeat, outperform or overcome an adversary. Often our greatest adversary is ourself. As U.S. Olympic gold medal skater Bonnie Blair puts it, "Winning doesn't always mean being first. Winning means that you're doing better than you've ever done before."

Winning is not about being the most talented, it's about being the most competitive, the most determined. Winners are those who understand commitment, who embrace their dreams and discover their abilities, who set a goal and find a way to do better than they've ever done before.

## Women Who Won

I've been in the business of branding for most of my professional life, beginning in 1981, when I was hired into Anheuser-Busch's Brand Management group. Working at a Fortune 100 company, where I had the opportunity to learn from some of the brightest marketing minds of the time, provided me with invaluable knowledge and experience. Since leaving the corporate world in 2003, I've expanded my branding practice to focus more on the human element of branding, and in particular, on coaching and building *personal brands*.

In 2017, I was asked to give a workshop on Personal Branding for Women in Business. In preparing the course content, it dawned on me how many of the people I featured in my weekly blog, Friday's Fearless Brand, were women.

As I began reviewing these subjects, all of whom were powerful, inspiring, and highly accomplished women, I realized that there was no single classification for these high-achievers. They included women of all ages—both living and deceased. There were Christians, Jews, Muslims, Hindus and Buddhists, and they represented almost every race and came from countries around the globe. Yet there was one thing they all had in common.

## These women had won.
They had accomplished their dreams, goals and desires regardless of the hurdles they faced. Not one of them had achieved that success without overcoming major challenges along the way. Those hurdles were many and varied. Many were based on gender, some on religion or race, while others reflected strong cultural bias.

Reading once again about those women made me think of my mother, Wilhelmina Aspasie Pecot Ellis—"Billie", to her friends and family. Starting in her earliest years and persisting throughout adolescence and adulthood, she faced profound challenges. She accepted what she had to, fought what she could, and used her talent, intellect, determination and big heart to raise a family, be a partner to her husband, and help thousands through her volunteerism. Billie knew who she was and what she wanted from life, the value she added and how she was relevant.

## Billie Ellis was truly a fearless brand.
She and the women in this book—and countless others who are not included here—are the examples that I want my twin

granddaughters—Abigail and Audrey—to know about, learn from and use as inspiration. I hope that many other women will gain insight and courage from these women who won, and that many more men will recognize the powerful and important roles women play in this world. Here's to universal understanding that the increasing contributions of women translate to a better world for us all.

I look forward to seeing both Audrey and Abby pursue their dreams, accomplish their goals, and become women who won.

# My Why

## Billie, Abigail and Audrey

*"At the end of the day, don't forget that you're a person,
don't forget you're a mother, don't forget you're a wife,
don't forget you're a daughter."*
**Indra Nooyi**

### Billie

Gabriel (Gabie) Pecot was the deputy sheriff in Charenton, Louisiana when he and his wife, Cecile, welcomed their youngest child into the world. Wilhelmina (who would be known as Billie) was born on September 16, 1924. She was the youngest of six children – four girls and two boys.

Charenton is a quiet town in Southern Louisiana boasting the beauty of the bayous, wildlife and moss-covered cypress trees. There's also no shortage of heat, humidity and mosquitoes. Some would find it to be a very tough life. So much so that the town was named after Charenton, France – a city best known for its insane asylum. An early French settler had declared that "anyone choosing to move to that part of Louisiana belonged in Charenton!"

However, for Billie and her siblings, a challenging life wasn't defined by nature. Rather, their challenges came in the form of personal tragedy and turmoil. Cecile died when Billie was just a year old. That left Gabie to raise six children while continuing as deputy sheriff. He would remarry, perhaps too quickly as that marriage ended in divorce.

Children are resilient, and Billie was no exception. When she was 13 years old, Billie moved to the big city of New Orleans. She lived with an older sister, graduated high school at the age of 16 and eventually took employment at the New York Life Insurance Company. Before long, she met a tall, handsome former football star—a student at the Loyola University School of Dentistry. Their attraction was immediate and strong.

Billie and Dave married when his stint in the Army was completed. They moved to Franklin, where Dave opened a dental practice. It was there that they had their first child, a girl named Sharon. Soon after, the Army contacted Dave, soliciting him to re-enlist. That's what he did.

A career in the military includes multiple moves – uprooting families, changing schools, adapting to new environs and making new friends. Billie would not allow those moves to be disruptive to her family. It was she who would coordinate the moves, organize schools, arrange living accommodations and basically, keep her family's life as normal as possible.

A move to Germany was especially taxing for Billie for a variety of reasons. To begin with, this would be a three-year stint. The family's goods needed to be sorted into groups for storage, shipment and checked baggage. At the time, she had four kids, three under the age of seven. She was pregnant with her fifth child and the two middle kids had come down with the measles. For Billie, it was just another move—the challenges didn't faze her.

She and Dave had five children in all—three daughters and two sons—their birth places a reflection of the family's extensive travel. Two were born in the United States, one born in Asia, one born in Europe and one born in the middle of the Pacific Ocean on board a military transport ship.

After living in most places no more than two or three years, Dave retired from the military and the family moved to his hometown of New Orleans. There, he became a professor at the LSU School of Dentistry. Billie continued to manage the family finances, kids' activities and schooling—which by then included researching colleges. As the kids left the nest, one after the other, Billie turned her energy to volunteerism, mainly at East Jefferson Hospital where she was named Volunteer of the Year on more than one occasion.

Billie had gone through most of her adult life with the knowledge that she had a rare form of leukemia—one for which there was no cure. Billie and the doctors never lost hope that a cure would be found before the disease fully manifested. Sadly, that didn't happen. Billie died on October 21, 1992.

I tell this story because Billie was my mother. As a child, I didn't appreciate the role she played in our family's life—and in mine. It's common for children to under appreciate their parents, to take them for granted, to have a sense of entitlement.

That begins to change with age and shifts even more dramatically as the child becomes a parent. Such was the case for me. Her strength, determination, caring, will and loyalty became even more apparent once she died. When it comes to my mom, the saying "you don't know what you've got 'til it's gone" comes to mind.

It took nearly two decades after her death for me to realize that Billie Ellis, my mom, was the first fearless brand I'd ever known.

*"We must tell girls their voices are important."*
**Malala Yousafzai**

## Abigail and Audrey

For most, July 26, 2011 was just another Tuesday. For a small group in St. Louis, it was a day of excitement, joy and blessings. That was the day that Abigail Joann and Audrey Sue made their appearance in the world. The twin sisters were two months premature—each weighing less than four pounds.

The girls had the good fortune to be born at a leading Neonatal Care Hospital—their home for the next two months. Abby and Audrey received top-level health care. They also received an outpouring of love from parents, grandparents, family and friends. Audrey and Abby were not only adorable, they were tough little girls.

They accepted the incubators, tubes, stethoscopes and constant monitoring without a care. There was no incessant crying or fussing, just two girls comfortable with their life and surroundings.

Today those girls are six-years-old. When Abby and Audrey completed kindergarten (they both love school), the girls, and their entire class, were asked what they aspired to be as adults. Abigail stated emphatically that she aspired to be a painter.

Audrey is motivated to become a ballet teacher. They are curious, intelligent, innocent, trusting, caring and bright girls. They have been named the cutest girls ever—by me.

Abigail and Audrey are my granddaughters. To me, they represent hope for the future—their young hearts and minds capable of so much. I want them to have every opportunity possible to follow their dreams and achieve whatever they pursue.

The twins will never meet Billie, their great-grandmother, but they will hear about her. They'll also hear about other strong, powerful women to whom they are related—they'll meet many of them. Abby and Audrey will hear about women who have accomplished things that no one thought they could—women who refused to be bound by cultural, societal or physical challenges. The twins will learn that while the path may not be smooth or easy, there is no reason why they shouldn't achieve great things and ultimately, become women who won.

# Ellen DeGeneres

## Harness the Power of Authenticity!

Until the age of thirteen she had lived a quiet life with her parents and older brother in Metairie, La.—just outside of New Orleans. The family—Christian Scientists—attended weekly services together. There, the signs on the wall touting the Golden Rule—treat others as you wish to be treated—left a lasting impression on her. She had a deep rooted love for animals—all animals—and briefly considered a future as a vet. While she didn't go out of her way to be funny, she noticed that people around her laughed—a lot.

Somewhat abruptly things changed—her parents divorced. Her brother, Vance, stayed in Louisiana with their father while she moved with her mother to Atlanta, Texas. She used her knack for comedy to keep things light and help her mother through that difficult stage. Her mother remarried, introducing a stepfather into her life—a man who secretly molested her.

She graduated high school, moved back to Louisiana and enrolled at the University of New Orleans. Her talent and passion for comedy moved her to leave school to pursue that career path. Things, once again, were going well—her comedy was being well received as she worked to hone her craft. She found love. Once more things changed—an auto accident took the life of her love.

The tragedy sparked a monologue called "A phone call to God" which she performed as emcee at a New Orleans club. From there she traveled all over to play at clubs, small bars—even restaurants. Her commitment—and her talent—paid off when in 1984 she was named the Funniest Person in America by the Showtime Network.

As a young comedian, she would watch the Tonight Show and tell herself that not only would she be on the show, she would be the first female comedian called over to speak with Johnny Carson. Years later—in 1986—that exact scenario played out. Her career continued to gain momentum—and in 1994 she landed the lead role in a sitcom named for her. It was wildly successful—she won an Emmy for writing, three Golden Globes and five Emmy nominations for outstanding lead actress just from this show.

Once more, things were about to change. Even with her tremendous success, she realized that she wasn't being totally authentic—so she did something about it. On April 17, 1997 she was featured on the cover on Time magazine announcing that she was gay—the first openly gay television star. Her character on the show followed suit shortly thereafter—an episode which drew over 42 million viewers. Conversely, the network promoted the show less, various groups called for a boycott by viewers and in 1998 the show was canceled.

Losing everything has its silver lining—it gives one time to reflect. She noted that nothing about herself had changed—yet everything else did. The reward was quickly apparent—she could now live with the gift of being completely herself—every day. Her career was impacted, but not destroyed—not by any means.

Today she has the number one ranked daytime talk show. She's won twenty-five Emmy wins, People's Choice and Teens Choice awards, Producers and Screen Actors Guild awards. She's had several movie roles both on-screen and as voice characters. She has hosted both the Emmy and the Oscar awards shows. She is one of the most popular talents in the entertainment industry.

These awards and accolades are quite impressive but they aren't what defines a fearless brand. They are the *result* of Ellen DeGeneres embracing her passion and honing her immense talent—but most importantly, her success has exploded exponentially because she had the insight and courage to be authentic.

## Fearless Brands live the adage "To thine own self be true."

Currently Ellen's show—aptly named The Ellen DeGeneres Show—continues to top the daytime ratings. She is the face of Cover Girl. She is the host of a new reality television show which focuses on interior design—a passion of hers—which she has produced and launched. She holds the record for having posted the most retweeted Twitter post in history—a group selfie taken as host of the Oscars. Her fun side really came out that night when she ordered pizza to be delivered to the entire audience. Ellen DeGeneres is a beloved celebrity and truly a fearless brand.

Ellen's path to stratospheric success has not been an easy one—there were major challenges throughout her journey. There's very little doubt that she will face even more challenges as she moves forward. What impresses about DeGeneres is how she has handled those situations. Throughout her life she has had the ability to realize that what's done is done—she has learned the lessons and has been able to turn her attention and effort to the future with a positive outlook.

The greatest gift she's given herself—and in turn to all of her millions of fans—is allowing herself to be herself—to be authentic. She was able to free herself of the secrets which held her from being completely genuine. She eventually told her mother about being molested. She 'came out' in a major way—being on the cover of *TIME* magazine will certainly destroy any secrets. Ellen knows that she is a comedian who just happens to be gay.

What really makes, defines and differentiates Ellen? When asked about her greatest attribute her answer isn't that she's funny or talented or popular—it's that she is kind. The signs on the wall of her childhood church made an impression—she lives the Golden Rule. She's funny, quirky, silly, loves to have fun—and she's kind—and that brings her greatest satisfaction.

What should you learn from Ellen when building your own fearless brand? It's rather simple—

**Be authentic!** – The absolute core element of any successful brand—any fearless brand—is authenticity. Embrace who you are, what your company or product or service genuinely are. Free yourself from any secrets.

**Create an emotional connection** – Authenticity guarantees that you will be able to connect with the people, prospects, fans or customers you are trying to reach. Those are the ones who define your brand. They'll know if you're genuine and relevant—and they'll know equally well if you're not.

Not everyone reading this post is going to be a fan of Ellen. Some won't find her funny. More won't be able to accept that she's gay. But *everyone* can—and hopefully will—learn from her experience, her actions, her success and her happiness. Want to be a fearless brand? Be kind. Dance a little. Laugh a lot. Above all—be authentic.

# Maggie Doyne

## 29-Year-Old Mother to Fifty, World Changer, Hero

Maggie and her two sisters, Kate and Libby, grew up in Mendham Borough, New Jersey. Nancy, their mother worked in real estate—their father, Steve, was a stay-at-home dad. After graduating from West Morris Mendham High School, Maggie embarked on a gap year. The purpose of a gap year—typically the year between high school and college— is to allow the individual to experience the world—to deepen practical, professional, and personal awareness.

Maggie left home with a ruck sack and a sense of adventure. Her travels led to several unique experiences. She lived in a Buddhist monastery, helped to rebuild a sea wall in Fiji and traveled to India. There she worked at a children's home serving Nepalese refugees. It was there that she met Top Malli, a Nepali working at the home. He and the other refugees had fled the brutality of a 13-year long civil war. That conflict had just ended, when Top decided to return to his home country—Maggie chose to travel with him.

Less than a year earlier, she had been a typical American high school student. What she experienced in Nepal would change the course of her life—and that of thousands of others. She witnessed poverty, starvation and people—mainly women and children—struggling just to survive. Maggie witnessed children hammering on the big rocks in a dry river bed in order to break off smaller stones which they would then sell. One of those kids, a 6-year old girl named Hima, would touch Maggie's heart. Maggie determined that she would provide schooling for Hima.

There were many more children that needed help—kids whose parents had been killed in the war or were incapable of helping. Maggie contacted her parents and had them wire her $5,000 savings, earned from babysitting jobs while in school. She used that money to buy a small parcel of land on which she built a house for herself, Hima and other kids she had taken responsibility for.

It was 2007. Maggie was 19. She was determined to make a difference. Her first step, together with Malli, was to create a non-profit foundation, BlinkNow. To be successful, she knew that it would be critical to engage the local Nepalese people. Shortly thereafter, the Kopila Valley Children's Home opened. A school which accommodated 400 students followed. Next would be a health clinic and a women's center. Nepali people comprised 90% of the staff—many of them orphans themselves.

In addition to Hima, Maggie would become mother to 51 children. The Kopila Valley structure would expand to four stories— large enough to provide safe and comfortable space for kids ranging in age from 1 to 19 years old. To be clear, it's not an orphanage—it's a home. Maggie created a family atmosphere—the children have chores, meditation time and importantly, a place where they belong. In addition to studies, students at the school participate in sports, community projects and are able to just be kids.

Because of her efforts—more correctly the results of her efforts—Maggie received the Forbes Award for Excellence in Education in 2013. She was honored by the Dalai Lama as an Unsung Hero of Compassion in 2014 and in 2015, she was named 2015 CNN Hero of the Year. The results are phenomenal—the accolades impressive. All of this is the result of Maggie Doyne being a fearless brand.

## Fearless Brands take action that makes a difference

Maggie Doyne, not yet 30, has made significant and positive impact in the world. Her foundation, BlinkNow, continues to thrive, as does the community it supports. They recently purchased a new property to create a totally green and sustainable 'off-the-grid' campus. They've converted to solar power.

Two factors may be most responsible for the continued success of this social enterprise. First, Maggie was determined to create a sense of family, filling a major void in the lives and spirit of an entire region. Second is the involvement of the local Nepali people, a strategy which Doyne adopted from the beginning and to which she remains fully committed.

There's much to learn from what Maggie Doyne has created—and how she's gone about making her vision a reality.

**Know your purpose** – Maggie Doyne set out as an 18-year-old to help others and experience life. She had no idea where that would lead. For Maggie, seeing the devastating impact of a war embodied in a 6-year old orphan girl, crystallized her purpose. For Maggie, meeting Hima crystallized her purpose. Knowing and embracing your purpose is essential to achieving your goals, adding value and enjoying the satisfaction that brings. You also need to realize that there is no specific timeline to finding your purpose. For some, it becomes clear early in life. For most of us, however, it's a longer journey—one which requires experience, failure and determination. Be diligent. Be open.

**Your team must share your values** – Maggie Doyne and BlinkNow are very direct about how different and difficult life is in Kopila. They do so intentionally, first to scare off people who may not be able to adapt. Secondly, they want to ensure that they only attract people who truly embrace their purpose and that are committed to respecting the local culture. The same thinking must be applied to your business. Be certain to have a process to attract and hire only those people who fit your company purpose and culture.

**Don't force your beliefs when collaborating** – As Doyne said in an interview with CNN—"I learned very early on, from the beginning, that I couldn't come in and just be like, "Here, I have a vision. This is what we're going to do." That doesn't work. It has to be slow; it has to be organic. And it has to come from the community and be a "we" thing." What works in one culture may not work at all in another. This is true as it pertains to countries and businesses. Starting with a self-righteous and closed attitude is a quick path to failure.

Maggie Doyne has been named a Hero of the Year. You and I may never achieve such an accolade—at least not on a global scale. However, we can be the Hero of the Year in our world. Follow Maggie's example. Find your purpose, no matter how long it takes. Focus on how you can add value to others. Trust the process. Be a fearless brand.

# Dafna Michaelson Jenet

## It Takes a Little Crazy to Make a Difference

Do you know someone who is always busy? The kind of person that actually makes you a bit tired just by hearing about all their activities and interests and such? If you do, this Friday's Fearless Brand will remind you of them— at least to a degree. If you don't know someone like that, you're about to. Meet Dafna Michaelson Jenet. She first and foremost is a mother and a wife. She's been married for two years to Michael Jenet. Between them they have three children along with all of the activity and chaos that entails. On top of that she is a speaker, a teacher, a storyteller, an author, a radio host, a blogger and a non-profit leader.

If you've been following this series, you'll not be surprised at this statement. None of that is what makes her a fearless brand— all of her activities, her accolades and her accomplishments are the result of her being a fearless brand. This blog is rather long— too long for some—so here's the essence of today's message.

## A fearless brand is built on a platform of authenticity— derived from clarity—resulting in conviction.

Dafna adds transparency to this 'formula' which increases her impact exponentially. It is her conviction that has allowed Dafna to pursue her vision of changing the world by building community.

The way she defines this is "Changing the mirror we use that reflects who we are as a society". This sounds like a fairly ambitious and lofty ambition...one which drew great skepticism from many—at least early on. It is her transparency that allows her vision to touch literally tens of thousands of people - providing hope, strength, optimism and a sense of community.

I first met Dafna in 2009 when she was in St. Louis as part of the Missouri leg of her **50 in 52 Journey**. As a single mother of two she came to realize that her professional path at the time was not her calling. The work she was doing wasn't her vision. Here's where conviction becomes a driving force in her life. Realizing that she needed to be authentic in her life's pursuits, she quit her job, cashed in her 401K and set off to visit each of the fifty United States—in one year. Her purpose was to find the individuals at the core of moving America forward. The unknown, unheralded people that were the soul of our country. Each weekend for a year, with the support of her then boyfriend Michael, she visited a different state discovering amazing stories of people making a difference in their community.

The next time we were together was at the Extreme Business Makeover conference in Orlando. At that time Dafna was planning her book and speaking engagements to deliver the results from her journey. As an aside, she also tweeted that entire conference almost verbatim which taught me a terrific social media tool—the magic of 'retweeting'.

Then life threw another challenge her way. Dafna was diagnosed with breast cancer. This was a journey no one wants to take yet one that thousands face every year. Dafna determined that the best thing for her was to share her experience to help others as well as herself. She began a blog. She shared the progression of her condition, her treatments, the double mastectomy, the resulting complications and her ultimate victory over the disease.

During that time she continued to travel and to speak. She started a radio show in Denver. She was the driving force behind the creation of TEDxCrestmoorPark. She also joined a mastermind group which I was a part of and we became accountability partners.

Since then she has gotten married and renewed her efforts at The Journey Institute. She has developed a white paper on her next big vision which she calls **Love Thy Neighbor**. She still teaches social media at MSU Denver, is very active in her faith on a national level and seemingly never runs out of energy.

This year, at the age of forty, she became pregnant. She and Michael were to have their own child—their little Peanut. An amazing dream come true which resulted in boundless joy for them and for so many. She began to share her experience of what it was like to be expecting at forty—primarily to help other women.

I cannot begin to imagine the anguish and pain and shock that Dafna and Michael experienced when at fifteen weeks they lost Peanut. Very few people can. There are so many more questions than answers for parents and family at a time like that. Once again, Dafna determined that she had to be both authentic—and transparent. She began to blog about Peanut—the baby never born. She wrote for herself—but she wrote for countless parents and siblings who suffer the loss of a baby and have no place really to turn.

She determined that Peanut's life need not be in vain. To spread hope and help and to be true to her vision of building community she and Michael are creating The Peanut Project. This initiative will provide information and education, a call center, clergy and non-faith based services to those in need.

Dafna is as authentic as one can be. She is more transparent than most could ever be. Her conviction is to help build a better world one person - one community at a time. As I told her, she is using her fearless brand to help our society become a fearless brand as well.

## Addendum

Dafna chronicled her 50 in 52 Journey in a book titled – *It Takes a Little Crazy to Make a Difference*. Published in 2015, the book recounts the stories, people and adventures of her year-long odyssey. That book won the International Book Award for Social Change.

She continues to be a woman with seemingly endless amounts of energy. Consider her list of volunteerism. She currently serves on the Adams County (Colorado) Youth Initiative board, The Commerce City Quality Community Foundation, The Carson J. Spencer suicide prevention foundation and Playworks Colorado. Dafna also serves as a mentor for City Year, Goodwill, and Junior Achievement where she teaches in a girls' and a boys' juvenile detention facility. Dafna is currently participating in Leadership Commerce City - a program of the Adams 14 Foundation. Recently, Dafna also completed a Civil Rights Leadership Fellowship with the Anti-Defamation League.

On top of everything else on her agenda, feeling the calling to make a difference through politics, she entered politics for her first time, bidding to become State Representative for the

Colorado House District 30. Running as a Democrat, she received a personal endorsement from President Barack Obama. (Regardless of your politics, it's very impressive to be acknowledged by a sitting President of the United States!). No surprise—she won and was sworn in on January 11, 2017.

In her inaugural session, nine bills passed of the eleven which she sponsored or co-sponsored—an 82% success rate. Those bills supported veterans, mental health and health care, education and disability law. In addition, she introduced 6 resolutions and held twelve town hall meetings.

The best advice that I can offer for those who aspire to be a fearless brand in the spirit of Dafna is this—know that your efforts and passion can effect change. Embrace your purpose, add a little bit of crazy and charge ahead at top speed. It's certainly worked for Dafna.

# Ingrid Vanderveldt

## One Woman Will Empower
## One Billion Women Entrepreneurs

Ingrid, born in Bethesda, Maryland in 1970, was one of four children. Her father worked in technology, having earned a PhD in Electrical Engineering—her mother had a Master's in business. It came as a surprise to her parents when the principal of Ingrid's school phoned to inform them that she had a learning disability and was failing third grade—he actually described her as retarded.

Her parents refused to accept that assessment, believing that their daughter merely needed more focus and attention. After researching things, they sent Ingrid to a different school a good distance away from their home—one which would provide a more productive environment for her to learn. They had also discovered that the school district was obliged to provide bus transportation for Ingrid, even though she was the only student attending the new school. As a result, Ingrid had a full-sized bus dedicated just to her.

Other kids would tease her, but rather than get down, she focused on the positives in her life. She had parents who believed in her and were encouraging, her own bus and a great deal of one-on-one time with teachers at the school—her take away was simply "Boy, am I special!" Eventually, it was discovered that her learning challenges were the result of poor hearing, having nothing to do with any sort of learning disability. Once that was addressed, she went back to her original school where her scholastic performance was impressive.

She went on to earn two Masters' degrees, the second one was an MBA from the McCombs School of Business at the University of Texas. That was in 1996. Having been entrepreneurial from a very young age—selling candy and lemonade—Ingrid embarked on developing her business idea. One thing she knew was that to be successful, one had to be open to asking for help—and that's what she did. She sought guidance from George Kozmetsky, the co-founder of Teledyne, the onetime dean of the McCombs School and the man who had mentored Michael Dell.

Ingrid had a vision for a data-mining and data-analytics built on a truly unique concept. It took nine months of hard work, learning, trial and error, direction from Kozmetsky and her practice of meditation, but eventually, things came together. Presenting the concept to an investor resulted in an offer of $2,000,000 to buy the company outright. She turned it down. Eventually, she did sell that company...but would go on to build and sell several more.

In 2011 she attended the second annual Dell Women's Entrepreneur Network event in Rio de Janeiro. She was struck by several thoughts beginning with how Dell supported entrepreneurs. Added to that was her belief that entrepreneurs would be the force which would turn around the global economy. For that to happen she knew that a new perspective was needed—it would be essential to leverage the eyes and talents of women. Flying back to the U.S., she relied on her practice of meditation to settle the thoughts racing through her mind. It was on that flight that she discovered her life's purpose.

She would empower one billion women entrepreneurs by the year 2020. For many, the idea of such a massive undertaking would be dismissed—but not by this fearless brand. Everything she had accomplished in her life was because Ingrid Vanderveldt is a fearless brand.

## Fearless Brands are driven by purpose and hard work

Ingrid Vanderveldt had already accomplished more than most entrepreneurs—male or female. In spite of that, she knew at her core that her life's work would be dedicated to making her vision a reality. Once back, she contacted Michael Dell with her ideas. Together with Dell's President, Steve Felice, Ingrid created and assumed a new position at Dell—Entrepreneur in Residence. In that position, she oversaw entrepreneurial initiatives worldwide helping to build a $250 million business segment and founded the $125 million Dell Innovators Credit Fund.

What best defines Ingrid Vanderveldt is that she is the founder and chairman of Empowering a Billion Women by 2020 (EBW2020). She is leveraging every bit of her life-long learning—beginning with her childhood businesses and scholastic challenges continuing through her role with Dell and her many companies. She is committed to providing women in business around the globe with the tools, technology and resources that all successful leaders and entrepreneurs require.

The same characteristics that make her a fearless brand, the same traits that will lead to Vanderveldt accomplishing her goal are concepts which you can—and should—embrace as you build your fearless brand.

**The Power of Belief** – Ingrid was wrapped in the power of belief beginning at a very young age. Her parents believed in her. Her experiences instilled in her the power of belief. It's that power which has helped fuel her success throughout her entire life. It's the power of belief that will drive her to make her vision a reality. The question is this—Do you embrace and possess the power of belief? It's essential to believe in yourself, your talents, your potential and your purpose. Surround yourself with people who believe in you. Lean on them when your own belief falters—and it will.

**The Power of Planning** – Perhaps it's Ingrid's first major business initiative that will best demonstrate the power of planning. She started with an idea—she lacked the knowledge and expertise needed to make it a reality. Ingrid opened herself to receiving help. She used that help as she planned—and learned—and ultimately found success. Planning has led to Ingrid's success as it will for you. Be humble enough to seek the expertise you lack.

**Get really comfortable with being uncomfortable** – To some, being uncomfortable is not natural and they strive to stay firmly in their comfort zone. Yet being uncomfortable is as natural as breathing. Take a look at lobsters. As they grow, their shells become confining—uncomfortable. When the shell gets too restrictive, they shed it and grow a new one—bigger, more comfortable. That process repeats time and again. The same idea holds true for entrepreneurs and in branding. Discomfort is necessary for growth and success. The choice is to become comfortable with the process or give up on growth.

I have no doubt whatsoever that Ingrid Vanderveldt will achieve the objective of EBW2020. Why? She is a fearless brand—she's embraced her purpose, she has the skills needed and the openness to seek help in those areas that she lacks. Importantly, her efforts are wrapped in relevance—to her, to women, to the world. You too can be a fearless brand. Find your purpose. Dream big. Use your talent and seek help as needed. Be relevant. You too can have a big impact in your world.

# Elisabeth Kubler-Ross

## How One Woman Shattered Paradigms
## of Gender, Dying and Grieving

Death was a distinct possibility for Elisabeth from her very first breath. Born in Switzerland in July of 1926, she was the oldest of three sisters. The triplets were born minutes apart from each other and each girl weighed only about two pounds each. The fact that each of the girls survived and grew up healthy is arguably unbelievable. Elisabeth was not only healthy, she was smart, driven and curious.

From a very young age, she developed an interest in becoming a doctor. Her father, however, had a different perspective—one quite common at the time—which was that Elisabeth could become a secretary in his business...or become a maid. Elisabeth would have nothing to do with those options.

Instead, she left home at the age of 16, working at a variety of jobs along the way. When World War II broke out, she volunteered at hospitals helping refugees. After the war, her volunteerism took her to several war-torn communities. It was as a result of this work that she came to experience the Majdanek concentration camp in Poland. It was a place of death where Nazis killed thousands of Jews. Yet Elisabeth saw a different perspective when she entered a room where the images of hundreds of butterflies had been scratched and carved into the walls by those facing death. That image would significantly influence her throughout her life.

She went on to study medicine at the University of Zurich, met and married an American medical student named Robert and moved to Long Island in the United States in 1958. Four years later the couple moved to Denver to teach at the Colorado University of Medicine. Through her studies and practice in medicine, Elisabeth had become increasingly aware of how little was known, much less taught, about the people dying and how to care for them.

When a friend asked her to substitute teach one of her classes, Elisabeth did so in a most unusual way. She invited Linda, a 16-year-old girl with terminal leukemia, to attend the class. Students were encouraged to ask Linda about her feelings and expectations about dying. It didn't take long for the girl to erupt in anger at how impersonal the questions were. She went on to explain what it was like not to dream about growing up, going to college, having a family or even going to the prom. That session had an effect on the students, but an even greater impact on Elisabeth.

Elisabeth became an instructor at the University of Chicago's medical school, where she continued to focus on dying patients. As the result of countless interviews and research, she came to create the five stages of dying—denial, anger, bargaining, depression and acceptance. This model was first delivered in the book *On Death and Dying. LIFE* magazine did a feature story which generated an immense amount of positive and grateful response from the public. The medical community and the faculty at the university had a differing perspective, which prompted Elisabeth to pursue private practice.

Over the next four decades, Elisabeth went on to author, or co-author, over twenty books, her last being *Of Grief and Grieving*. She earned twenty doctorate degrees, was named in 1999 by TIME magazine one of 'The Century's Greatest Minds' and in 2007, she was inducted into the American Women's Hall of Fame. Not to be overlooked is that Elisabeth is credited with beginning the modern-day hospice system. Each of these accomplishments alone is noteworthy, when combined, these results can only be attributed to the fact that Elisabeth Kubler-Ross was a fearless brand.

## Fearless Brands pursue their purpose with unwavering passion and determination.

Elisabeth Kubler-Ross is arguably one of the most influential contributors to all of humanity in the twentieth century—and beyond. Her unwavering determination and passion have had a significant impact on how society as a whole, and the U.S. in particular, think about death and the dying. Her unrelenting pursuit of her dreams and her interests, in the face of serious obstacles, has helped to empower an entire gender. Her glass ceiling covered the basement—by shattering it, she opened countless floors for women worldwide.

The Kubler-Ross scale of dying, helped to quantify a subject mostly avoided before her efforts. The dying were ignored or patronized. Their care was provided from the thinking of the living—without understanding of the needs and wants of the dying. Elisabeth helped to change that thinking. She did so in spite of a father who had limited perspective on the role of women. She did so in spite of a medical community filled with skepticism—happy to continue on in ignorance. She did so in spite of critics who questioned the 'science' at the very core of her work.

Kubler-Ross did extend her learning to a study of the life after death and spirit channeling. Many used that pursuit to call in to question her work on the five stages of grief and dying. There will always be skeptics—Elisabeth carried on in her pursuit of knowledge in spite of them all.

One thing cannot be disputed—Elisabeth is a fearless brand—offering a great deal for us all to learn about our own brands:

**Follow your own path** – At the core of fearless branding is authenticity. At the core of authenticity is being true to oneself. Kubler-Ross chose to follow her own path from a very early age. There was no chance that she would succumb to the life of a maid or secretary merely because it was her father's direction. Later, she would refuse to back away from her study of death and the dying merely because it made many of her peers uncomfortable or skeptical. For all of us to become a fearless brand—to be authentic and content— we have to find the courage and determination to follow our own path regardless of obstacles.

**Clarify as needed** – Many took the Kubler-Ross scale as a literal sequence, one which they felt 'tucked messy emotions into neat packages.' As friend and co-author David Kessler puts it, "...the five stages help us to frame and identify what we might be feeling. There is no typical response as there is no typical loss." If your message is misunderstood—or if it has evolved—clearly and quickly communicate its meaning. Clarity is power—it enlightens those we serve as well as ourselves.

**Keep learning and evolving** – From helping the sick and injured to studying the dying and death to an interest in the afterlife and the spirit world, Elisabeth never quit learning. She was a 'seeker' throughout her entire life. Her pursuit of knowledge and her openness to new concepts are what helped her to be such a powerful contributor to the world. That same pursuit will continually add value to you and your brand—thereby providing greater benefit to those you serve...and let's face it, that's what branding is all about.

You may not have known about 'fearless brand' Elisabeth Kubler-Ross but you likely have heard of the five stages of grieving. They apply to death, divorce, business setbacks, losses by sports teams and so much more. Her efforts, at least indirectly, opened countless doors for women. Will your brand have such far-reaching impact? It certainly can. There is no reason that it cannot—so long as you stay true to yourself, create and communicate great value and adapt as needed to new circumstances.

# Isabella Springmühl

## She's More Special than Special Needs

Guatemala is, in many ways, the hidden gem of Central America—sandwiched between Mexico to the north, Honduras and El Salvador to the south and Belize to the east. The Guatemalan people are friendly and hard-working. The country has a diverse culture, with a rich Mayan heritage—it's home to Tikal, the ancient Mayan 'city in the jungle'. In spite of poverty and high crime, Guatemala has a unique colonial charm.

Guatemala is also home to Isabel Tejada and her four children—the youngest, Isabella, was born on February 23, 1997. Typically, the 'baby' of the family is considered special. This was true with Isabella in more ways than one as she was born with Down Syndrome. She would be called Belita, a nickname for Isabella which means 'Little Beauty'. Her mother would come to appreciate what a special gift Isabella would become in her life.

From an early age, her mother noticed her flipping through fashion magazines, looking at the clothes and tracing the pictures. Beginning at age 6, Isabella began to create outfits for her rag dolls—using bits of fabric she would come across. Her oldest sibling was her only brother. He would come to adore her and watch out for her. He found some of her writings and had her read them to him. A talented musician, he used those words as lyrics in a song written just for her—a gift that would touch Isabella's heart.

Despite the challenges that come with Down Syndrome, Isabella lived a relatively normal childhood. She attended the local high school, graduating with all of her 'normal' peers. Her dreams of continuing on to university to study fashion were shattered when her admission was rejected based on her condition. Isabella made up her mind that she would turn that 'NO' into a big 'YES'.

With the support of her family and driven by her determination, she began to learn sewing, knitting and fashion design. She discovered that her grandmother had been a fashion designer, owning a studio called Xjabelle. Between that fact and her brother's musical talents, Isabella had no doubt that creativity and design ran in her genes.

The brightly colored fabrics created in Guatemala became the heart of her fashions. Isabella enthusiastically designed clothes for the mainstream population, but her greatest passion was to design clothing for people with Down Syndrome. Because of their unique physical composition, those with Down Syndrome have a challenge finding clothes to fit. Isabella was committed to offering solutions for that challenge.

Isabella started her own company which she called Down to Xjabelle—to acknowledge her condition and to honor her grandmother. In addition to clothing, she began to design bags and jackets. Her bold designs, use of vibrant colors and intricate embroidery earned Isabella the chance to display her designs at the Museo Ixchel, Guate Extaordinaria. Her clothes sold out.

In 2016, Isabella became the first designer with Down Syndrome invited to display her work at London Fashion Week. At the age of 19, she was also one of the youngest designers to be featured. Her designs received rave reviews—as did Isabella herself. Her designs are merely a reflection of the girl—bold, determined, lively and so very special. Isabella was included on the BBC 2016 list of 100 inspirational women. These results are due to the fact that Isabella Springmühl is a fearless brand.

## Fearless Brands are not limited by age, physical condition or discrimination

After London Fashion Week, Isabella went on to showcase her "peace and love" collection in Rome. At the age of 20, Isabella Springmühl's future is as bright as her smile and the Mayan inspired fabrics she uses in her designs.

Isabella is not just a fashion designer on the rise—she is a true example of what can be accomplished with an attitude of "Why not me?" Fueled by her talent and intense passion, she refused to be derailed from her dreams. To put it in her own words:

*"Sometimes it takes us people with Down Syndrome more effort, more energy, but at the end, we can do it. Have dreams, and make them come true...see me? I am doing what I dreamed."*

There is something truly powerful and much to learn from a person so young in years yet so advanced in perspective.

**Embrace your dreams** – Some say find your passion—others, like Simon Sinek, say discover your 'why'—still others simply call it their drive. Dispensing with semantics, it comes down to your embracing dreams. Isabella knew that—she embraced her dream and is living a life of fulfillment and happiness. Her dream, in turn, is helping to inspire others. Dreams can do that—embrace yours!

**We define ourselves** – Isabella was refused admission to university, as well as two fashion schools, based solely on what others deemed was not achievable for a person with her 'condition'. Isabella would have none of that—no one else would define her. No one else would tell her what she could or could not do. She knew that she was a talented and driven fashion designer—who just happened to have Down Syndrome. Heed others' advice and input—but it's up to you to define who you are, what you can do, what you will do.

**Strive to be 'carefree'** – Isabella describes her fashions as "...carefree, just like me!" Being carefree does not mean that you don't have issues and challenges in life. It's more of an attitude. 'Belita' lives life on life's terms. She is happy as she says to "learn from the University of life" and experience all that she can. The very simple formula for being carefree is to accept what you cannot change but change what you can. It works for Isabella and it will work for you as well.

Isabella Springmühl is deemed special needs by many people. In reality, she is merely special. Special in her attitude, her actions, her determination, her talents and her dreams. It's what makes her a fearless brand. Those same attributes will allow you to also be a fearless brand. Be your special self.

# Dame Stephanie 'Steve' Shirley

## Meet Steve—The Most Fascinating Woman You've Never Heard Of

Refugees, in order to survive, have been forced to flee their countries throughout history. Such was the case with five year old Stephanie and her 9 year old sister who fled Nazi Germany in 1938. Born of a Jewish father, their mother put them on a kindertransport, a train for children refugees that would take them from Vienna to England. They weren't alone—nearly 10,000 primarily Jewish children—were welcomed into the United Kingdom.

Stephanie, of course, had no understanding of what was going on, what this England place was or why she and her sister were sent there. What she came to realize is that the foster family who took them in, helped save them from the holocaust. Even at a young age, this fact would have a major impact on Stephanie's life. Having been saved through the generosity of total strangers, she became determined to show that her life had been worth saving. That she would certainly do.

She had an interest in science and a particular passion for mathematics. Those subjects weren't readily available to females in those days—but she was determined to pursue her desired studies. Performing well on assessments, she was allowed to take several courses in math and science at the local school for boys. Upon graduating, she went to work rather than pursue a university education given the limited science curriculums available.

Instead, she went to work at the Post Office Research Station. There, she helped to build computers from scratch and programmed them using machine programming. At the same time, she pursued a mathematics degree in night school. She moved to the private sector, going to work for CDL Ltd., a computer development company. It was there that she first experienced the 'glass ceiling'. It was the 1950's. She would not tolerate being hugged or pinched—behavior that was deemed 'normal' at that time. More so, she realized that she had advanced as far as she ever would—entirely because of her gender.

By 1962, she was married, and with the full support and encouragement of her husband, decided to start her own business. Her concept was truly unique and well ahead of its time. Her company would sell software, a concept considered foolish by most. In those days, software was given away as an inducement to purchase the hardware. Stephanie knew there was an evolving need for custom software. Hers would be a company of women—bright, talented and smart—who, like herself, stayed home to raise children. With that, she launched Freelance Programmers. She pioneered flexible scheduling and embraced a 'trust the staff' approach.

As a female, she faced challenges which no male had to deal with. After discussion with her husband, she began to use the name Steve in her business dealings. Letters were answered. Doors were opened. The surprise that he was a she, quickly evaporated when business needs were met. The company's output required extensive coding. Programming was in its infancy at that time which resulted in the company and its employees becoming coding trailblazers. It was this team of women that created the first 'black box' for the Concorde.

Stephanie—Steve—decided to give 25% of the company to her staff, at no cost to them. In 1975, Britain passed an Equal Employment Opportunity law, which had the ironic consequence of forcing Steve to hire men—but only highly qualified men. The company continued to grow. By 1996, this female owned company started with 'bizarre concepts' was valued at $3 billion. Seventy of the staff had become millionaires as the result of the ownership stake they were given. Those results were realized because Dame Stephanie 'Steve' Shirley is a fearless brand.

## Fearless Brands are both determined and persistent

What an incredible legacy Dame Shirley would have created if the story were to end there—it doesn't. Steve, as she very comfortably goes by today, was nowhere near finished with her life's purpose. She and her husband had a son, Giles. At the age of two and a half, he changed into an unmanageable toddler and lost what little speech he had. It was then that Giles was diagnosed as profoundly autistic.

Giles became the first resident in the first house in the first charity that Steve created. She became a pioneer in the development of services to support autism. She went on to start more homes, schools, research facilities—whatever she could do to fill any gap in services for the autistic. Most recently, she's started a three year think tank on autism. Giles died in 1998. Steve's love for her son and her commitment to address the impact of autism have not—and will not—waver.

The Oxford Internet Institute (OII) is another of Steve's initiatives. Its mission is to study the social, economic, legal and ethical ramifications of the internet. OII is a department of the University of Oxford which is committed to the social science of the internet and is focused on research, teaching and policy.

Today, Dame Shirley is 82 years old. Her determination and persistence are as strong as ever. She is truly a fearless brand and someone from whom we can learn a great deal

**Embrace what drives you** – Dame Shirley enthusiastically embraced her new country, becoming a patriotic citizen of Great Britain. She has an appreciation for the generosity of strangers and a country which open its arms to people in need which as she says "Only someone who's lost their human rights, can understand". She was able to discover her purpose in life at a very early age—to prove that hers was a life worth saving. Do you know what drives you? Do you know your purpose? If so, embrace it every day—if not, find the key which will unlock that power.

**Make yourself invaluable** – She half-jokingly says that she has no fear of ever being lost, because if she went missing "several charities would quickly come to find me." Be so committed to what you do—to your purpose—that your absence couldn't go unnoticed. Doing so isn't difficult when you know your purpose—when you embrace your passion.

**The magic is in making things happen** – Ideas are great says Steve. What's essential, however, is making it happen. That takes a relentless energy, strong self-belief and determination. It requires courage and a willingness to accept failure on your path to success. If you know your purpose, but aren't 'making it happen', you need to either reignite your energy or redirect your efforts.

What an amazing gift the world received when a young refugee was welcomed by a country and embraced by strangers. You can't replicate exactly the ground-breaking and innovative path that Stephanie 'Steve' Shirley blazed. You may not become worth $1.5 billion or even live to 82 and beyond. But you can learn from her, adopt her traits, be inspired by her and build yourself into a fearless brand.

# Liv Boeree

## Are You Willing to Gamble on Yourself?

Known as the Garden of England, Kent is a county known for its gentle hills and sea lined borders. It touches Greater London to the North as it is located in the South East of England. It is famous for the White Cliffs of Dover, Canterbury and Leeds Castle to name but a few points of interest.

It is where Olivia grew up—climbing trees, playing with her dog, racing birds—basically enjoying life in the country. Perhaps her greatest love was riding and competing in horse shows, an interest she inherited from her mother. She participated in every sport while in school, but her primary focus was on learning. She was especially drawn to science, math and geography and it was those subjects which she chose to study at "A-Level"—think honors classes, courses which universities use to measure a student's potential.

Having earned A's in every one of those courses led to her being accepted at the University of Manchester. There, the tree-climbing, horse riding girl studied Physics—and Astrophysics. The girl was brilliant and driven. There was yet another side to Liv (as she had come to be known)—she discovered she loved metal. Music—not the elements. While continuing to perform at a high academic level, she also played electric guitar in a garage band known as Dissonance.

Graduating with a First Class degree (again, think honors level), Liv decided to take a gap year before entering the prestigious University College of London, one of the top schools in the world. A gap year is common in the UK. It is a year that students take to grow, mature, learn and experience life. Many take a year off, some work, while still others hike across South America. Liv worked a bit and modeled a little before deciding that her best path was to audition for game shows. Seriously.

After advancing through the entire casting process for a show, the concept of which was kept secret, she was selected to be one of five contestants. The show? Teaching five complete novices how to play and compete in the game of poker. Her math skills and her solid thinking prepared her well and her performance reflected that. Drawing pocket aces, the best start to a hand, she was certain she was on her way to winning the show. It was then that she discovered the difference between certainty and probability.

Losing, she was devastated. One of the professional poker players acting as a coach on the show was the world ranked poker star, Annie Duke. Duke consoled Liv and helped her to understand the concept of 'emotional control'. Liv was hooked on poker. In the face of a concerned mom and stepdad and a disappointed father, she chose to pursue professional poker rather than continue the path of a rocket scientist. She also wouldn't become a rock star, but she could live the rock star life in the world of poker.

She became a hostess on a British poker television show. That introduced her more readily to the world of poker and many of its best players. As she played more and more, her skills improved. Her first significant win earned her $30,000. In April of 2010, she won the largest ever European Poker Tour event in San Remo. That pot was $1,700,000. To date, she has earned well over $3,000,000 playing poker and is one of the top players in the world. In so doing, she has met her love and soulmate (another poker player) while also meeting every one of her Metal music heroes. She has also started *Raising For Effective Giving* (REG), a movement to raise money within the poker industry which will support specific charities.

Accomplishing all of this, living such a full live—all by the age of 31, is the result of Liv Boeree gambling on herself and becoming a fearless brand.

## Fearless Brands gamble on themselves

Liv "the Iron Maiden" Boeree is certainly a fearless brand. She has a broad range of talents, gifts and skills—smart, logical, fun-loving, courageous, caring and bold. She found her passion in many endeavors—horse riding, math and sciences, music and modeling. She's found her purpose in Effective Altruism.

Poker requires one to be logical, to assess the odds, to read one's opponents and to make the best decision possible based on a combination of intellect and 'gut feel'. Liv realizes that the very best poker players lose, at a minimum, 95% of the time. That's an awful lot of losing. One of the keys to success, learned early on from her mentor Annie Duke, is the art of detachment. The concept is simple—don't get hung up on the thought of losing. Rather, evaluate your performance—take whatever lessons there are to be learned—move on.

She brings that same philosophy to her charitable efforts. Effective Altruism is simply the process of evaluating all charity options, determining which ones provide the greatest good based on performance and put your money there. This removes the emotional aspect of giving and, as in poker, focuses on the greatest percentage of winning.

There's so much to learn from Liv Boeree—this 31 year old fearless brand.

**Gamble on yourself** – Liv Boeree isn't a gambler because she is a poker player—she plays poker because she's a gambler. She's gambled on herself her entire life. She gambled by placing her scholastic endeavors in STEM courses (science, technology, engineering, math). Result? A First Class degree from Manchester. She gambled her gap year on pursuing a game show. Result? A career which incorporates her every interest. To become a fearless brand—you must gamble on yourself. Assess the odds, factor in the intangibles then make your play.

**Diverse interests rock** – Astrophysics, horse riding, gambling, heavy metal music and philanthropy may seem disparate. However, for Liv, embracing all of her interests make her the complete person that she is. It's not mandatory to drop an interest or two in order to pursue your main profession. Quite the contrary, your diverse interests compile to make you who you are. Embrace your interests, your skills, your talents. Together, they make you a more complete and stronger person

**Give with purpose** – Liv's belief in Effective Altruism reflects a very logical and reasoned approach to giving. There are independent groups which evaluate charities eliminating all emotion. Those charities are targeted by Liv's REG program. Regardless of your method, be a giver. Give value—always. Give time and money to others in need—to others who are in position to extend help. Define the purpose which best suits your beliefs—just give.

Will you become a world-class poker player? The chances are very slim if you're at a table with Liv Boeree. Will you become a fearless brand? The chances are excellent if you learn from Liv. Embrace your passions. Discover your purpose. Engage and improve your talents. Give. You'll realize results which fulfill your very soul.

# Dr. Hayat Sindi

## Dreams of Science and the Science of Dreams

Dreams. We all have them. Some are discarded as wishful thinking. Others are wrecked by a litany of roadblocks—some real, many perceived. Then there are dreams that explode into reality—crashing through all obstacles—in spite of nearly impossible odds. That type of combustion doesn't happen spontaneously—ignition and fuel are required. Ignition comes in the form of inspiration. The fuel is a combination of determination, commitment, and talent.

As a child, Hayat, one of eight children in an average family, loved learning. Her school days were the happiest days of her young life. She was particularly enamored with scientists—finding them confident and innovative. She was especially taken with the impact their work would have in the world. The dream of becoming a scientist was born.

Hayat approached her father to share her ambition of becoming a scientist. She was convinced that he could teach her anything she wanted to learn. His advice was supportive and direct, telling her that with education and learning, she could become anything—she could become a scientist. Sounded simple.

However, Hayat faced nearly impossible odds. She was born in Mekkah, Saudi Arabia. Cultural beliefs and tradition presented very limited opportunity for advanced education for a female. Hayat would not be deterred. With her family's blessing, she set off to London to pursue her education. A Saudi girl, not yet twenty, traveling on her own to a different country, was anything but the norm. Adding to the challenge was the fact that Hayat didn't speak a word of English.

The admissions clerk at the University of London told Hayat, through an interpreter, to go back home—that her idea was crazy. Instead, Hayat became determined to learn English. She watched the BBC network, studied hours on end and eventually was accepted to King's College of London where she earned a degree in pharmacology. There was pressure on her to abandon her religion and cultural beliefs, along with her traditional Muslim dress. Hayat refused to submit to the pressure, stating that one's religion, gender or color weren't factors in her professional pursuits.

Hayat was accepted to the Cambridge University biotechnology doctorate program—the first Saudi women to do so. By 2001, Hayat had become the first woman from an Arab state to earn a PhD in the field.

Earning her doctorate was not the end of her dream. Her goal all along had been to better integrate science with society. Hayat pursued science for the sake of humanity—which is what led her to biotechnology. She envisioned science becoming more accessible, affordable, and easy to use. Improvement in diagnostics became her focus. Frustration became an early byproduct. She struggled with how to move science from the lab to a product. Her lack of understanding when it came to business was one more hurdle. Another hurdle meant one thing—one more solution was needed. Hayat enrolled in the Harvard School of Business.

Hayat went on to become co-founder of Diagnostics for All, offering cost-effective diagnostic tools for people and geography outside of traditional medical care. Their diagnostic patch, made of paper at a cost of less than a penny, provides quick and affordable assessment of liver issues—saving tens of thousands of lives. She has been recognized numerous times winning awards and honors that include, the Honorary Global Thinkers Forum Award of Excellence in Science and was named a 2011 Emerging Explorer by the National Geographic Society. CEO magazine has named her the 9th most powerful Arab woman and the 3rd most powerful Saudi Arabian women. She's was appointed by UNESCO head Irina Bokova as a UNESCO Goodwill Ambassador and was part of the first group of women to serve in Saudi Arabia's Consultative Council. These accomplishments—having her dream come true—are the result of Dr. Hayat Sindi being a fearless brand.

## Fearless Brands pursue their dreams with determination, inspiration, and talent

Dr. Hayat Sindi has faced—and overcome—more obstacles and challenges than most people can even imagine. She has faced cultural bias, language barriers, gender bias, and more. Her integrity has been challenged—falsely. Accusations and rumors have swirled around her—initiated by close-minded, cultural conservatives seeking to derail a successful woman—a scientist.

Dr. Sindi refused to have her dream smashed. She launched the i2 Institute of Imagination and Ingenuity whose mission is to to create an ecosystem of entrepreneurship and social innovation for scientists, technologists and engineers - its primary focus being on youth, both male and female.

Her dream began at a very early age. To make that dream a reality, Dr. Hayat Sindi educated herself, overcame all challenges, and maintained her determination and persistence. Dr. Sindi has never lost sight of her primary goal of using science to create sustainability, fight poverty and address climate change. Her dream is now reality because she is a fearless brand - one from whom we can learn a great deal.

**Find a mission in life and contribute something to humanity** – Dr. Sindi is driven to contribute to humanity. She has broken barriers between East and West, smashed cultural stereotypes, led the development of technology which saves lives and empowers people. It's that mission—that dedication to enhancing humanity—which fuels Dr. Sindi. We all have a mission—it's a matter of discovering what that is. Each of us can positively contribute to society as we pursue our mission and realize our own dreams.

**Focus on relevant factors** – Gender, color, religion and race aren't factors when it comes to capability and potential. We need to remain focused on truly relevant factors. Doing so allows us to commit 100% of our energy and effort to realizing our dream. Doing so keeps us from diminishing our impact.

**Embrace your dream** – We all have dreams. It's up to us to embrace them—to commit to them—to put forth the effort required to make them a reality. The mere pursuit of our dreams will fuel us—motivate us—drive us. When you know your dream—embrace it. You might not impact the entire world—but you'll certainly impact *your* world.

Dr. Hayat Sindi is a truly fearless brand. Her drive and commitment, her effort and talent, her belief in humanity all contribute. Those traits exist in each of us—it's merely a question of how big you want your dream to be.

# Diane Hendricks

## Shattering Norms, Hard Work and Determination Yield Powerful Results

Diane Smith was born into a Wisconsin dairy farming family in 1947. She was one of nine children—all girls. When she was nine the family moved to a several hundred acre farm in Osseo, Wisconsin. Diane wanted to spend her time outside and had no qualms about working on the farm—but that wasn't an option. Her father believed that females were not meant to do farm work—common thinking for the times. She may not have agreed, but she accepted that's the way it would be.

While a student at Osseo-Fairchild High School, she became pregnant by her first love—she was 17. She got married and had the baby—it was what her parents thought was the right thing. She and her husband moved to Janesville, WI where he worked for Chrysler Motors. Diane went to work for Parker Pen. It didn't take her long to realize that she had no interest in being a factory worker. Within three months she began selling new construction.

She began to study to become a real estate broker, even though her job didn't require her to be licensed. Part of what drove her was a determination to be self-sufficient—to be able to support herself and her son. Once she turned twenty-one, she filed for and received a divorce.

She met Ken Hendricks, a roofing contractor, when he phoned her in an effort to arrange a date with her for a friend of his. That call led to several others as they learned more about each other—realizing that they had a great deal in common. The blind date never happened—but a relationship between Diane and Ken did. They were married in 1975.

Prior to that, they had begun to work together, buying, rehabbing and selling homes in Beloit, WI. Ken wanted to become a distributor. In 1982 they pooled their savings, drew on the equity in their homes and used a line of credit to buy three roofing stores. That was the beginning of American Builders and Contractors Supply Co. Diane and Ken proved to be a dynamic business team, leading ABC Supply Co. to tremendous success.

Ken and Diane were also a dynamic couple—together they had seven children. Then tragedy struck. Ken and Diane were having extensive remodeling done at their home. One evening, while checking on the progress of that project, Ken fell through a poorly marked opening in the roof and died from his injuries.

Diane was devastated. A company approached her in an effort to buy the company, assuming they could get a very favorable deal in the face of Ken's untimely death. Proving her business prowess, her determination and her business smarts, Diane flipped the script and bought the suitor. She had resolved to continue the business she and Ken had built.

Today, ABC Supply Co. has over 600 stores in the United States with revenue estimated by Forbes to be $5.3 billion, making it America's 74th largest privately owned company. ABC

Supply has been the recipient of the Gallup Great Workplace Award the last five consecutive years, which honors the most engaged and productive workforces in the world. These are clearly powerful results—results which can be traced to the efforts of a fearless brand—Diane Hendricks

## Fearless Brands combine talent with determination

Diane Hendricks was determined to become self-sufficient from a very young age. As a child, she was prohibited from doing work on the family farm based on accepted norms. As an adult, she refused to let those beliefs hold her back. Diane Smith Hendricks achieved unparalleled success in an industry predominantly run by men. Her intelligence, experience and determination allowed her to break through barriers—real or perceived.

ABC Supply's success has been achieved through organic growth and key business acquisitions. A cornerstone of that success is the list of core values developed by Diane. Adhering to these values is one key reason that ABC Supply has won the Gallup Award so often. In addition to ABC Supply, Diane heads the Hendricks Holding Company, comprised of some 30 companies whose business includes insurance, manufacturing and logistics to name a few.

Some might be surprised that Diane Hendricks in number one on Forbe's list of America's Richest self-made women, surpassing such notables as Oprah Winfrey and Meg Whitman. What doesn't surprise anyone that knows her is that Diane Hendricks is very active in civic and philanthropic endeavors, as well as a variety of community organizations.

There is much to learn from Diane Hendricks, as evidenced by the results she's realized as a fearless brand.

**Don't be limited by societal norms** – It is clear that Diane Hendricks has succeeded in spite of the restrictive beliefs common during her childhood. Not only did she shatter any constraints, she did so in a male dominated industry. The simple lesson here is be true to yourself. Follow your aspirations—don't be the victim of subjective barriers. Blaze your own path.

**Be determined** – Hendricks faced challenges throughout her life—challenges which could have prompted her to give up, to throw in the towel. She refused to quit. When Ken died, she faced what might be her greatest challenge. Wrapped in grief and shock, she could have taken the easy route and sold to that suitor. She determined to continue her dreams. Determination is a mark of a fearless brand.

**Pass it on** – Another mark of fearless brands is their propensity to be positive contributors in their community and beyond. Whether what you pass on is monetary, opportunity, environment or knowledge, share the fruits of your efforts. Don't think of this act as a debt or an obligation. Know that it is an opportunity to add value to others—to add good to the world.

Chances are you've not heard of Diane Hendricks. Widespread fame is not essential to being a fearless brand. The success she's realized—the results of the Diane Hendricks brand—can be replicated by everyone, regardless of celebrity or extreme wealth. Achieving the success of your dreams, while not easy, is simple. Find your purpose, use your skills, blaze your own path, be determined and pass it on.

# Lolo Jones

## Overcoming Life's Hurdles— Achieving Personal Victory

Lori was born in Des Moines, Iowa in 1982—one of five children of an inter-racial couple. Her family was poor, in large measure because her father spent a good deal of time in and out of prison. For all intents, Lori's mom was a single mother who did whatever it took to care for her children. With little money, the family moved often—so much that Lori went to eight different schools in eight years. There were times her dad showed up having purchased a clunker of a car, which, without fail would break down.

When that happened on cold nights, he would tell Lori they would run home to stay warm in the cold Des Moines nights. Lori fell in love with running—it became the friend that never left. Running was the only constant in her life. Growing up, she learned what it meant to fight for everything in life. She learned to shoplift—not for the latest fashion, but for food to eat. For a period, she, her mom and siblings stayed in a church basement compliments of the Salvation Army.

Lori found some stability as a student at Roosevelt High School. She joined the track team, volunteering to run hurdles when no one else stepped forward. She excelled at track—both sprints and hurdles. Kim Carson, a Roosevelt alum, had achieved great success running for Louisiana State University. Kim became aware of Lori and recommended her for a scholarship to the LSU track coach, Dennis Shaver.

Shaver had his doubts about the level of Lori's talent—could she make it at LSU, a school whose female track team had won the national championship eleven years in a row. He offered her a scholarship based on the traits she showed—organized, motivated, goal oriented, enthusiastic. Shaver was the rock-solid, positive male figure Lori had never before known. He was her coach, her mentor, her father and her friend. By the time Lori graduated, with an Economics degree, she had become the number one ranked female hurdler in the country.

It was 2004 and she tried out for the U.S. Women's Olympic team. Failing to qualify, she sat on her couch, crying, as she watched the Games on television. Things were different in 2008. She had become the number one ranked hurdler in the world and a heavy favorite to win Gold in Beijing. She advanced through the qualifying rounds with relative ease. Then it was her day—the race for gold. She streaked down the course, clearing hurdles and breaking in to the lead. Suddenly—disaster. Lori's toe clipped the ninth of ten hurdles—she stumbled and finished seventh. Her dream of winning Olympic gold for herself and country instantly shattered.

To see her live interview with Bob Costas the next day, one would never know the loss and pain and angst that Lori felt. Her strength of character summed up in this quote "In 2004 I cried on my couch. In 2008 I cried on the track, In 2012 I'll cry tears of joy in victory."

Lori had lived a life filled with hurdles before she ever stepped foot on a track. She learned early on that those hurdles needn't turn into failure—rather, they were learning opportunities. She went on to be a three time Olympian, a three time World Champion and an American record holder. Today she is still a professional athlete, a spokesperson for Red Bull and Asics and a celebrity known throughout the world. Those accomplishments are amazing. They only occurred as the result of the efforts of a fearless brand—Lori "Lolo" Jones.

## Fearless Brands face their hurdles, converting them into positive experience

Lolo is a woman of intelligence, talent, beauty—and a very unique name. Her mother is also a Lori. When people would ask for Lori the question became Big Lori or Little Lori—Little Lori morphed into Lolo. She stands out partly because of those attributes, but what best defines Lolo is her character, conviction and sense of self.

Her Olympic loss was devastating, but she wouldn't allow that to define her. When she raced again, she clipped more hurdles—something that had never happened so consistently in her career. It turns out that Lolo had an issue with her spinal cord—hers was much lower than normal and was placing great strain on the nerves to her legs. Her brain would tell her foot to lift but had no idea where the foot was. Lolo underwent a successful operation to clip the affected nerve, recovered faster than any other patient and got back to training.

She made the Olympic team once more in 2012, finishing in what many consider the worst spot possible—fourth—no medal. Again, she pressed on. In 2014, she became a member of the U.S. Women's Bobsled team and competed in the Winter Olympics, her third. Again, there was no medal. Again, there was the pride of having given her best and representing her country.

Lolo receives a great deal of grief and chiding because she is very open with her Christianity. She is also open about being a virgin, and remaining that way until she is married. Many scoff at the attention she receives having never won an Olympic medal, yet Lolo remains true to herself—her standards, her beliefs and her personality. There is much to learn from Lolo and her experiences.

**Adversity is a given, make it a positive!** – Lolo had a childhood which stacked the odds against her graduating college, much less achieving world-class success and being a global celebrity. She is open about her childhood, not for sympathy, but because it was a never ending learning experience. She learned to be a fighter—to not quit. She learned that hurdles could either hold you down or lead to great success. Look for the positive, learn the lessons, fight the fight, strive to succeed.

**Adapt to your environment but remain true to yourself** – Her childhood certainly had its challenges but it was when she went to college that Lolo had to adapt in a totally different way. She had grown up in Des Moines, a quiet city with Midwestern values and a predominantly Caucasian population. Suddenly she was in Baton Rouge with its Southern culture, abundant seafood and a much more diverse demographic. Lolo showed how to adapt—how to integrate her personal brand into her new setting. Situations change. You need to adapt to new environments without compromise—be true to who you are.

**Acceptance, Courage, Wisdom** – There has been no shortage of things in Lolo's life beyond her influence—poverty, injury, defeat—things which she had to learn to accept. She also knew that much could be changed and that she would find the courage to do just that—education, training, dedication. More often than not, she has done a good job of knowing what to accept and where to change. She found mentors to advise her. She used her experience to make decisions. Put your efforts behind things which will yield results—don't waste time addressing matters which you can't affect.

Lori "Lolo" Jones has achieved things very few ever will. She has handled disappointment and devastation in a way most can only hope to replicate. As you seek success—as you look to improve in life and 'upgrade your brand' learn from Lolo Jones. Face life's hurdles head-on. Don't let them keep you down. Learn from them. Be a fearless brand.

# Amara Majeed

## How Amara Majeed Found the Courage to be Authentic

Her parents had immigrated to Baltimore, Maryland from Sri Lanka. Formerly known as Ceylon, Sri Lanka is an island nation just south of India. Despite a civil war which raged for over 30 years, ending in 2009, the nation is a peaceful blend of cultures and ethnicities. There is a rich heritage of Buddhism, by far the most prevalent religion, yet there are significant numbers of Hindu, Muslim and Christian, primarily Roman Catholic.

The family heritage was Sri Lankan, but she was born in Baltimore, where she was raised along with two older brothers. Throughout school she was diligent in her studies, driven to learn and determined to be successful. As with any normal girl her age, she laughed with her friends, talked about boys and became a huge fan of Taylor Swift and the TV show *Gossip Girl*. Things began to change for her around the time she began high school. It was then that she adopted the custom of her Muslim faith and began to wear a head-scarf, known as a hijab, when in public.

Most people began to look at her differently, to treat her differently and to keep their distance. She hadn't changed from the likeable, intelligent driven girl she had always been. Born and raised in the U.S., she only knew herself to be an American—appreciating the freedom and opportunities her country presented. Apparently, by merely wearing a head-scarf—a hijab—she felt some of that freedom compromised.

She was very intelligent—very well-read. There was no delusion on her part that her country had been very strongly affected by people of her faith—extremists—terrorists. She also knew that while it seemed that most terrorists were Muslim, the vast majority of Muslims were peace-loving and not terrorists. That fact was widely overlooked and the negativity that resulted was palpable.

What could a 16 year-old high school student do? Most would do nothing—not her. She believed that education and communication would help to eliminate some of the misperceptions. With that as her goal, she began an online initiative she called The Hijab Project. She created a website which encouraged women who wore a hijab to share their stories. She challenged other women to wear a hijab for a day and share their experiences. As a result of this effort, she was invited to the floor of the U.S. Senate to receive an official citation commending her project.

By the time she was 17, she had become a contributor to the Huffington Post. That was no easy feat—she had to persistently pursue that opportunity without being deterred by the many responses rejecting her proposal. She finally sent her story via email directly to Arianna Huffington, who embraced the talented, eager writer and activist. She subsequently became a contributor to CNN and Bustle. Also at 17, she wrote and published a book—*The Foreigners*—intended to eliminate stereotypes about Muslims.

Today she is an 18 year-old freshman at Brown University—where she studies pre-law and is perhaps the only student wearing a hijab on campus. She is perhaps most known for an open letter she sent to Republican presidential candidate Donald Trump after he called for a ban on Muslims entering the U.S. In that letter she provided her perspective on what it's like to be an American who happens to be Muslim. She went on to share her beliefs about the far-reaching and negative impact of his comments. To date, she has not received a response.

She has received media coverage including *The Washington Post, The Baltimore Sun*, ABC television, Global News and more. She was named one of the twenty most impressive high school students to graduate in 2015 by *Business Insider*. Named as one of the 100 Most Inspiring Women of 2015, she was featured in that season of BBC's "100 Women."

Those achievements and accolades are impressive, especially in that they have been accomplished by a woman who is just 18. Her age is not, however, what drove these feats. These are the types of results which come from building a fearless brand—and while that is not what she set out to do, Amara Majeed has done just that.

## Fearless Brands are built from displaying courage in the face of fear

From a very early age Amara Majeed's parents taught their children how 'lucky and privileged' they were to live in the United States. She discovered her purpose unexpectedly—as the result of practicing her religion. That purpose is to promote peace and harmony by building understanding and eliminating misperceptions about Muslims.

This post is not about religion. It is not about politics. It is about the powerful results realized by building fearless brands. Amara is quoted in a February 2015 Baltimore Sun article as saying "I want to transform myself into this concept of liberty and equality. People die, but ideas don't. I want my ideas to live on long after I've left this world." That thinking defines a fearless brand.

When it comes to building your own fearless brand, what can you learn from Amara's story?

**To thine own self be true** – The easier softer path for Amara would have been to simply stop wearing her hijab. Authenticity is at the root of every fearless brand. Self-integrity is the ultimate definition of authenticity. Be true to yourself.

**Courage is acting in the face of fear** – We all have fears—even fearless brands. Amara—and most American Muslims—live in fear every day. It's not about being fearless—it's about being courageous in spite of your fears. It's her courage which has allowed Amara to have such a far-reaching and profound impact.

**Don't quit, don't settle** – In that same Baltimore Sun article Amara Majeed states "I'm constantly trying to up my game," she said. "I want people to be able to look at me and know what I stand for." Branding is a never-ending process. There is always room to upgrade your brand—to improve your skills and recharge your purpose. Stay diligent. Seek to add value.

Amara Majeed is clearly an exceptional young woman, she has had more of an impact on the world by age 18 than most do in a lifetime. Let that inspire you. Find your purpose and pursue it with passion. Build your fearless brand. Celebrate the results that are guaranteed to follow.

# Jo Malone

## Smelling the Sweet Scent of Success—Twice

Joanne was born in 1963 and grew up in a council house in Kent, England. Her father, Peter, was a painter—her mother, Elaine, was a beautician. As a child, school was difficult for her as she was severely dyslexic. It was for a different reason, however, that she left school at the age of fourteen. She left school to work and look after her mother, who had suffered a stroke. She worked in a local floral shop as well as helping to keep her mother's beauty business viable.

Joanne loved the scents at the florist. At home, while working in the beauty business, she began to create her own fragrances combining various flowers with grated Camay soap. One of her creations was a ginger and nutmeg bath oil, which she began giving as a thank you to her customers. One customer loved the oil so much that she ordered 100 bottles to be used as place settings at a party she was hosting. Shortly after that party, 86 of the guests contacted her to buy more oil.

At 19, she had married Gary Wilcox. A surveyor, he quit his job to become Joanne's business manager. His business sense, combined with her talent for creating unique and appealing fragrances, led to the fast growth of the business. Gary found a retail location and they opened their first store at 154 Walton St. in London—it was 1993. On the first day the store was open, a man walked in offering Joanne 1 million British pounds for her company—she declined.

The business grew quickly. Joanne's scents—in candles, oils creams and more—were simple, incorporating only one or two scents. Soon the products were picked up by Bergdorf Goodman in New York City. Joanne had developed creme colored packaging featuring black ribbon and scented black tissue paper. Those boxes supported the positioning of her products—high-end, exclusive, special, and desirable. Her clientele included fashion industry insiders, celebrities, even royalty.

In 1999, she sold the business to Estee Lauder, after building a strong and trusting relationship over a period of three years. The sales price was "undisclosed millions." She stayed on as the creative director. Her new position included a great deal of travel, primarily to New York. She was very pleased with the manner in which Estee Lauder had embraced the brand, striving to maintain the qualities that first made it so successful. Things were going well...and then they weren't.

Joanne discovered a lump which led to a diagnosis of an aggressive form of breast cancer. The management at Estee Lauder told her they would take care of her—which they did. She flew to Sloan Kettering Cancer Center in New York where she underwent a double mastectomy and a full year of chemotherapy. Cancer beaten, she went back to work full-time but things had changed. She wanted to enjoy as much time with her husband and their then two year old son. In 2006 she had a very amicable separation from Estee Lauder.

Joanne had built what started as a hobby into a multi-million dollar global brand which had been purchased by the largest company in the beauty business. She had built a fearless brand combining passion with her unique talent to create luxury products desired by millions. That brand is eponymous with her name —Jo Malone. The story doesn't end there, however, as Jo Malone the *person* is the truly fearless brand and there was more for her to accomplish.

## Fearless Brands

Jo Malone had created a successful global fragrance line. She had left the business, but her name had not. Jo was very confident in the future of the brand she had built. She loved working with fragrances but her separation included a five year non-compete clause. She turned to another passion.

Jo started *High Street Dreams*, a show on BBC television which encouraged and supported small business and entrepreneurs. That show led to the successful launch of six new businesses in the UK—two of which continue to thrive. She also pursued her interest in food and cooking—another activity which exposed her to a myriad of fragrances. The urge to once again be active in the fragrance industry never left.

Once her five year hiatus was complete in 2011—she launched a new fragrance company. This one she called Jo Loves. Its red, white and black colors, the new fragrances and her business model are designed to be successful while having minimal impact on the Jo Malone brand. This company launched online—a real challenge for a fragrance company. A bigger challenge was to create awareness that Jo Malone—the *person*—was the heart and soul of this company.

Her ability to create unique and highly appealing fragrances has helped to let the industry know that Jo Love is Jo Malone's. Making the scents available was met in large measure when she and Gary opened their first store. They opened that store at 42 Elizabeth Street—significant because it was at that location that Jo had her very first job with the florist. Jo Love is all about memories so what better place for the store?

It's easy to see that Jo Malone the product line and Jo Malone the person are both fearless brands. So what can you learn from them?

**Fearless brands inspire** – Perhaps the greatest result you can achieve with your brand is to create an emotional connection with customers and employees. Emotion is at the core of our decision to buy—our sense of loyalty. Jo Malone the product begins with quality and is differentiated by its unique fragrances. Importantly, it meets the desires of its customers. The same holds true for Jo Malone the individual. Her passion for fragrance and meeting customers' wants are essential. What makes her more inspiring is her authenticity and humility. She is still the same person who began working at 14 to help her family.

**A brand is more than a name** – The name Jo Malone evokes thoughts of amazing fragrances, quality product, packaging and service. The name Jo Malone brings to mind a bright, smiling, positive, hardworking and talented businesswoman, wife and mother. Yes, the name is important—as a brand trigger. The heart and soul of all brands is the sum of their intangible assets...the emotional and intellectual perceptions we have when we experience a brand stimulus.

**Your personal brand extends to everything you do** — I'm often asked why I focus on the personal brands of professionals, business owners and their employees. I have found that Jo Malone's story answers that question clearly and effectively. Your personal brand is at the very core of your actions and contributions. There's a little bit of you in everything you do—including your professional life. You focus on your personal brand to bring your best to life.

There is a great deal to learn from both Jo Malones. If you take nothing else from this post I urge you to make it this—it's the intangibles that define your brand. Ask yourself—"Does my brand inspire the action(s) I desire?" If your answer is yes, congratulations. If it's no, which is a rather common occurrence, take heart.

It's never too late to pursue your vision of success. Follow the passion that inspires you. Build a brand that inspires action in others. Smell the sweet scent of success.

# Zaha Hadid

## Designing New Paradigms
## in Business and in Life

Zaha was born on October 31, 1950 in Baghdad, Iraq. Her family was upper-class and well-educated. Her mother was an artist—her father, a successful industrialist. He was also politically active, co-founding the liberal National Democratic Party. Her family was Sunni Muslim yet leaned towards Western multiculturalism.

Early in life, she attended a French-speaking Catholic school whose students included Christians, Muslims and Jews. Later she would attend boarding schools in both England and Switzerland. Her educational experiences provided a broad perspective across diverse cultures.

She was also strongly influenced by a trip her family took to tour Sumerian cities located in what was once known as Mesopotamia. The houses and buildings fascinated her—as did the wide variety of landscape. She realized that there was a 'flow' across the people, buildings, landscape—providing a sense of 'oneness'. The family home—one of the first Bauhaus-style buildings in Baghdad—would also influence her later in life.

Zaha would study mathematics at the American University of Beirut, Lebanon. It was there that she soon discovered her interest in architecture. That led to Zaha enrolling at the Architectural Association School of Architecture (AA) in London in 1972. AA is recognized globally as one of the leading schools for architecture. She earned her degree in 1977, going to work at an architectural firm in London before starting her own company.

Much like Frank Lloyd Wright before her, Zaha's designs were anything but 'the norm'—they were bold, innovative and truly unique. The family trip to Sumera fueled her belief that everything should flow together. Her concepts incorporated angles and curves which would combine to create breathtaking structures—if built.

Her ideas and designs were well received in trade magazines and architectural journals—but few became reality. The firm won several small projects. While her business continued to grow—albeit slowly—Zaha taught at the Architectural Association. She entered numerous design competitions—winning several while earning greater admiration within the industry.

Her first significant design was a fire station—featuring many unique angles—constructed in Germany in the early 1990's. In 1994, she entered—and won—a competition to design the proposed Cardiff Bay Opera House in Wales. When that result was overturned, she re-entered and won again. Zaha was devastated when the sponsor withdrew funding, effectively ending the project.

Rather than allow such a catastrophic event to deter her—she determined to press on. Interest in her work continued to grow and in 1998 she was commissioned to build the Contemporary Arts Center in Cincinnati, Ohio. Her creative use of limited space was fueled by her unique perspective of a structure's 'flow'—immersing the center's visitors into the art in a way never before experienced.

That building was a tipping point of sorts for Zaha—both professionally and personally. More sought after than ever, she was chosen to design a museum to adjoin the Price Tower in Bartlesville, Oklahoma which was one of Frank Lloyd Wright's notable designs. Her work had become widely accepted and appreciated. As such, she was chosen to design structures across the globe.

Personally, her success in business led to her becoming easier to work with—less caustic. Zaha faced tremendous challenges in a male dominated industry as a woman—and an Arab (Zaha had become a naturalized British citizen). In response to that resistance, she had become direct—even abrasive. That all began to wane as she became more recognized for being a bold and innovative force in architecture.

In 2004, she would become the first woman and the first Muslim to win the industry's top honor—the Pritzker Architecture prize. She would teach at the Harvard Graduate School of Design, the University of Illinois at Chicago's School of Architecture, the Hochschule für bildende Künste Hamburg. Her work is represented by some of the most unique and dynamic structures in the world.

These spectacular accomplishments are the result of Zaha Hadid being a fearless brand with a pioneering vision in her work and in life.

## Fearless brands have tremendous vision and persistence

Zaha Hadid died of a heart attack in 2016 while hospitalized with bronchitis in Miami, Florida. Her presence in the world will continue in the form of the buildings she designed—constructed, works-in-progress and yet to be built. Her creativity and boldness are evident not just in the structures themselves—but in their purpose.

This is evidenced by unique engagement of visitors at the previously mentioned Contemporary Arts Center. That same philosophy is evidenced in a BMW factory in Germany—designed in such a way that management and workers would encounter each other more often—within the natural flow of work.

Zaha Hadid was certainly a pioneer and innovator as an architect. Her approach to design, the paradigms she shattered and the success she experienced will have a long-lasting impact on architectural design. By example, the Opus in Dubai is a spectacular example of Hadid's work.

Her contributions to the world extend well beyond her many physical structures. She forged a new path for women—not just in architecture—but in a very broad sense. Women can exist and excel in typically male environs. With her success, Hadid has helped shatter stereotypical perceptions about Middle Eastern women. She has shown them to be intelligent, talented and able to make powerful contributions in business and in life.

There is much to learn from Zaha Hadid as a fearless brand.

**Dream, Dare, Do** – Zaha had many experiences as a child and young adult which shaped her dreams and would drive her success. She embraced her passion and realized that her purpose was to help redesign the world through architecture. That career path was daunting, yet she dared to follow it—to do whatever was necessary. Dare to embrace your dreams—do what fuels your passion and drives you.

**Gender? No problem** – With very few exceptions, women can flourish and succeed in any discipline. Sadly, it's a tougher road for women in some disciplines than it is for their male counterparts. Even in the face of greater challenges, woman can succeed. Zaha Hadid has proven that in her field—tens of thousands of women have shown the same in countless other fields. If you're a female, fight the good fight. If you're a male, embrace women's talent, insights and intelligence—it will make you a better person and build a better business.

**Bold can be beautiful** – Many people are too bold—many others are not bold enough. Zaha's success is the result of being bold in design, application and thinking. She wouldn't allow industry norms to restrain her imagination. Allow yourself to be bold.

What Zaha Hadid accomplished as a woman of Arab descent proves what can be accomplished when we combine our dreams and talents with determination. Learn from her experience—dream, dare, do—become a fearless brand.

# Pat Summitt

## How You Too Can Reach the "Summitt" of Branding

She was born in Clarksville, Tennessee, the fourth of five children. She grew up on the family farm with her three older brothers and younger sister. Farm life taught all of the children hard work, commitment and dedication. When their chores were completed, she and her brothers would play two-on-two basketball. She not only developed a love for the game, she learned how to hold her own against the boys.

However, she encountered an obstacle when she reached high school age—the local school didn't have a girls' basketball program. Her father was so supportive that he moved the family across the county line to Henrietta, Tennessee where she excelled on the girl's team. There was a new obstacle when it came time for her to go to college—scholarships didn't exist for female basketball. Her parents sacrificed to pay tuition, allowing her to attend the University of Tennessee-Martin.

Of course she played basketball for the UT-M Lady Pacers. As a junior, she played for the U.S. in the World University Games held in Moscow. She next set her sight on making the U.S. team in what would be the first ever Olympics to include women's basketball. Another goal—another obstacle. As a senior, she blew out her knee. Doctors told her she needed surgery and wouldn't be able to play again. She and her father had a different message for the medical team—they needed to 'fix her knee' because she was going to the Olympics in 1976.

It was then 1974 and she was offered the graduate assistant coaching position at the University of Tennessee—Knoxville (UT). Just as she accepted that position, the head coach unexpectedly resigned. As a 22 year old having never coached a game in her life, she was named the head coach. Most of her players were just a year younger than her.

In each of her first two seasons of coaching at UT, the team won 16 games—which was considered respectable although not championship caliber. Women's sports were barely funded at that time—she not only coached, she did the team laundry, drove the van to games and did every other task, no matter how menial. She also worked out twice a day, lost a good deal of weight and got her knee in game shape.

Suddenly it was 1976 and she was a player coach on the U.S. Women's Olympic team. That team went on to win the silver medal, a performance that would set the stage for a future of Olympic success for the U.S. women. Back at UT, she had no way of knowing that her first two seasons of coaching would be the only ones that a team she coached would win less than 20 games in a year.

As a coach, she incorporated the work ethic which she learned on the farm. She instilled in her players the determination that she had learned as a young girl playing against her older brothers. A life of overcoming obstacles, of finding a way to succeed, helped her teach her players how to win against the odds. Her teams went on to win eight national championships, sixteen SEC Conference championships and sixteen SEC Tournament titles. The University of Tennessee Lady Vols basketball program became one of the most elite programs in the nation for nearly forty years.

As a coach she compiled a record of 1,098 wins vs only 208 losses—a nearly unheard of winning percentage of 84%. She won countless coach of the year awards, most notably the Naismith Coach of the 20th century. Outside of basketball, she was awarded the Presidential Medal of Freedom in 2012. These accomplishments don't define the coach—rather these accomplishments are the direct result of Pat Summitt being a fearless brand.

## Fearless Brands see opportunities where others see obstacles

Pat Summitt discovered early in her life that she had a passion for basketball. She incorporated the lessons she'd learned on the farm into her basketball efforts—both as a player and a coach. She often told recruits "If you're lazy, stay away from me and my program—we work hard!"

Summitt had a trademark stare which she frequently focused on referees—but also on players, assistants and anyone else who didn't meet her expectations. As a coach, she also cared a great deal for her players, exhibiting a motherly side rarely seen by the public. What the public could see was her love for her son, Tyler, himself now a head basketball coach for the women's team at Louisiana Tech.

She is facing what is no doubt her greatest obstacle in her usual manner—with courage, dignity and determination. On

August 27, 2011, Pat Summitt courageously announced that she had been diagnosed with early onset dementia, "Alzheimer's Type," and that the 2011-12 season would be her last as the head coach of the University of Tennessee.

There was an immediate and profound outpouring of support and love not only from the UT community, but the sports world as a whole. A "We Back Pat" campaign sprung up seemingly overnight. In November of 2011, Summitt announced the formation of her foundation, the Pat Summitt Foundation Fund, with the proceeds going toward cutting-edge research.

While many saw her announcement as courageous, it was merely Pat Summitt being herself—transparent, direct and no-nonsense.

There is much to learn about building a fearless brand by getting to know Pat Summitt—principles which relate to any and all brands

**Don't quit on your dream** – Pat Summitt never met an obstacle which could hold her back. In every instance, she found a way to overcome the challenges. It's that determination which set the stage for her to fully develop her fearless brand and to achieve the results that effective branding yields. Know your purpose and don't give up on it.

**The dream is nothing without the work** – The accomplishments driven by Pat Summitt's passion only materialized because of her stringent work ethic. Know your dream, find your purpose—but do the work needed to make it a reality.

**Be genuine and transparent** – With Pat Summitt, there is no doubt as to her beliefs and her expectations. Not only is she totally authentic, she is transparent. She instilled those traits into her basketball program as well. She is a person of integrity and courage. She has run a program above reproach. Not only do you need to know your value—your brand—it's vital that your value proposition is completely and easily known by those you serve.

It's unlikely that most people will equal the same level of success and fame as Pat Summitt. The good news is that doing so is not a requirement for building a fearless brand. Embrace your dream. Discover your purpose. Know your talents—and improve on them. The formula is quite simple actually—deliver exceptional value—receive extraordinary results.

# Dr. Maya Angelou

## A Brand Uncaged—A Gift to the World

Marguerite Johnson was born in St. Louis, Missouri on April 4, 1928. She was three when her parents' marriage ended. Her father sent her and her four year old brother, Bailey Jr., to live with their paternal grandmother. Annie Henderson lived in Stamp, Arkansas where she owned a successful grocery store. What makes this scenario exceptional is that Mrs. Henderson, Marguerite and Bailey Jr. were black. It was the early 1930's—a time of overt racial discrimination. Annie instilled in her grandchildren the Christian principles of faith and love. She showed how to live with independence and courage.

When Marguerite was seven, her father showed up and took her and her brother back to St. Louis where they lived with their mother. Her mother's boyfriend raped her at the age of eight—he was tried but released. Two days later he was found beaten to death—Marguerite and Bailey moved back to Stamp—back to live with their grandmother. Marguerite was absolutely certain that her speaking of the rape had caused his death. With that belief, she didn't speak for over five years—essentially becoming a mute.

At the encouragement of a friend of the family, she began to read books by significant authors such as Dickens, Shakespeare and Poe. She also became aware of black female artists such as Anne Spencer, Frances Harper and Jessie Fauset. At the age of thirteen Marguerite began speaking again. Shortly after, the children moved to San Francisco to once again be with their mother.

Marguerite was awarded a scholarship to study dance and drama at the San Francisco Labor School. She dropped out and became the first African-American female cable car operator. At seventeen, she gave birth to a son whom she named Guy. Her mother, who had become a nurse, was the one who actually delivered the baby. As a single mother, Marguerite took a variety of jobs to support herself and Guy—waitress, cook—whatever.

Soon, her passion for the arts—performance, singing, dancing, poetry—began to call to her...and she answered. She had married in 1951—an interracial marriage that met with the disapproval of her mother and society as a whole. She danced professionally in clubs around San Francisco before her son and new husband moved to New York, where, she sang and danced calypso. Her marriage ended after three years, she then toured Europe in a production of Porgy and Bess.

Back in the U.S., she recorded a calypso album, joined the Harlem Writer's Guild and began writing an autobiography. Over time, she wrote and directed film and television and performed on Broadway. She heard Dr. Martin Luther King which motivated her to help start the Cabaret for Freedom to benefit the Southern Christian Leadership Council (SCLC), subsequently becoming its Northern Director. She became a passionate activist—anti-apartheid, pro-Castro and definitely in support of civil rights.

It was 1969 when her completed book—*I Know Why The Caged Bird Sings*—was published and received immediate acclaim. In it she portrayed her personal life, leaving nothing out. She wrote about the rape, the racism, the challenges, the victories, her accomplishments. One review said that in the book she wrote about "blackness from the inside without apology or defense."

She went on to write thirty-six books, seven of which are autobiographies. Her poetry is recognized around the world to the point that she's been called the Black Woman's Poet Laureate. She received the National Medal of Arts in 2000 and the Presidential Medal of Freedom in 2011. Her works, her wisdom, her talent, her beliefs have influenced literally millions of people across multiple generations.

All of these accomplishments are the result of a fearless brand—the incomparable Dr. Maya Angelou.

## Fearless Brands

Marguerite Johnson came to be known as Maya Angelou. Her beloved brother Bailey couldn't pronounce her name so she became 'My' or 'Mya' sister—Maya. She adopted the name Angelou early in her performing career because it was felt that it would be more distinctive and memorable than Johnson. Her name may have changed but Maya Angelou has been completely authentic from a very early age.

She learned that some things required acceptance—but that there was much which could be changed. Dr. Angelou learned to give voice to her experience, her beliefs and her wisdom through her actions, her writings, her activism and her talent. Her writings document history through her first-hand experience of life as a black woman, a single mother, fighting poverty, seeking higher education and empowering others.

Dr. Maya Angelou died on May 28, 2014—she was eighty-six. Throughout her life she was committed to learning and teaching. She never quit living with the courage and independence, the faith and love instilled in her by her grandmother. Fortunate for us, there are numerous lessons which we can learn from the life and teachings of Dr. Angelou.

**Don't be held down** – There were any number of conditions and situations which could have held Dr. Angelou down—but didn't. That's because she learned early in life to channel her efforts towards things she could change and affect—and to accept those things she had no control over. She would consistently seek options and solutions which allowed her to move in the direction she chose. Know your parameters but also know your opportunities—find the courage to change what you can. Dr. Angelou said it this way *"If you don't like something, change it. If you can't change it, change your attitude. Don't complain".*

**Use all of your talents** – Dr. Angelou believed that we do ourselves a great disservice when we limit our talent to one endeavor. The variety and diversity of her activities proves that we need not worry about becoming a jack-of-all-trades. Tap into your full potential. You may not be able to write poetry at the level of Maya, but you can indeed write good poetry. *"It is time for parents to teach early on that in diversity there is beauty and there is strength".*

**Treat people well** – Perhaps the most shared quote from Dr. Angelou is this *"I've learned that people will forget what you said, people will forget what you did, but people* *will never forget how you made them feel"*. Be certain that a component of your brand includes empathy and consideration of others' needs and wants.

For all of her eighty-six years, Dr. Maya Angelou continued to evolve her brand—adapting, exploring, pursuing, learning. Branding is a never-ending process. Your brand can always be upgraded. Be diligent. Be interested. Be teachable.

# Sara Blakely

## She Put Her Butt on the Line to Build a Brand

Born in 1971, she was raised in Clearwater, Florida. Her father would ask her and her brother the same question every night at the dinner table—"What did you fail at today?" One night she answered—"I tried out for a new sports team today...I was terrible!" Her dad responded with a big smile, an 'atta girl' and an enthusiastic high five. On those nights when she stated that she'd not failed at anything that day, the response was one of disappointment.

So it was that she learned from a very early age to embrace failure because it meant she was trying something new—that she was learning and growing. Accepting failure as an option allowed her to pursue her entrepreneurial spirit at an early age. One such endeavor saw her set up a haunted house at Halloween and charge the neighborhood kids to go through it.

As a teen, she experienced an inordinate amount of adversity. At sixteen, she saw her friend get hit by a car while riding her bike, and die. Also that year, her parents divorced. Soon thereafter, two prom dates died in separate incidents. She thought of her own mortality and used the realization that life can end at any moment as motivation.

Her father had given her the audio edition of Wayne Dyer's *How to be a No-Limit Person*. She listened to the ten cassette tapes so often that she memorized every word. Friends at school were hesitant to ride in her car because they knew they too would be hearing Dyer's tapes.

She went on to Florida State University where she graduated with a degree in legal communication—her plan being to become a lawyer like her Dad. She abandoned that idea when her answer to the question "What did you fail at today?" was the Law School Admissions Test (LSAT)—she failed it twice. Instead she went to work at Walt Disney World in Orlando—as a ride attendant. She endured three months at that job before answering an ad from Danka to sell fax machines door-to-door. By age 25 she had been named national sales trainer.

Invited to a party one night, she had decided to wear a new pair of cream colored pants, but was confronted with an age old problem—visible panty lines (VPL). None of her undergarments solved the issue. Not afraid of trying something new, she cut the feet off of a pair of panty hose and wore them under her pants. Problem solved—no VPL and she could wear her open toed shoes. Even though they ran up her legs all night, she knew the modified pantyhose presented a huge opportunity.

She moved to Atlanta where she continued to sell fax machines while spending all of her free time on product development—researching hosiery patents, seeking the right fabric and cold calling hosiery companies in nearby North Carolina. Her idea was rejected time after time, until one plant manager called her back. His two daughters refused to let him pass up this new product.

She had $5,000. She produced what she could and began to call on retail stores, eventually getting approval from Neiman Marcus to sell in a handful of their stores. She sent everyone she knew into the stores to buy her product—then reimbursed them. She went to stores herself and spoke directly to potential customers. She brought pictures of herself to show the difference between her product and traditional options. She sent a supply to the Oprah Winfrey Show and ended up being named one of Oprah's favorite new products in the year 2000.

Her research showed that many successful consumer companies had names which used the 'K' sound. Endless ideation sessions to find a product name proved fruitless. While driving one day, the name came to her—Spanks. She immediately knew it was the one—but she wanted to make it more memorable so Spanks became Spanx.

Today, the company produces $250 million in annual revenue. The product line has been expanded to include bras, panties, jumpsuits, shorts, leggings, jeans and more. They even make items for men. The girl who was taught to embrace failure, the girl who began entrepreneurial pursuits as a child, the girl who memorized every word on Wayne Dyer's tapes created what is now one of the most beloved companies in the world. This brand's stratospheric success is due directly to an individual fearless brand—Sara Blakely.

## Fearless Brands

In 2012 at the age of 41, Sara Blakely became the youngest woman ever to join the FORBES list of billionaires. She did so without an inheritance. She owns 100% of Spanx, which is debt free. She has never taken an outside investment and has spent virtually nothing on advertising.

In 2003 she auditioned for Richard Branson's reality show *Rebel Millionaire*. She finished as the runner up but gained immeasurable exposure for herself and Spanx. Importantly, she and Branson developed a keen friendship which continues to this day.

As a billionaire, there is very little that is typical about Blakely—but she's a very typical mom. Married with a six year old son, she volunteers at her son's school, drives a white Toyota minivan and she goes out after work for drinks with friends.

Blakely is firmly committed to helping women succeed in business. She travels constantly to give talks in which she shares the keys to her success while offering encouragement and support to women. A program called "Leg Up" was created by Blakely to help female entrepreneurs succeed in business. Participants receive one-on-one mentoring and product features in the Spanx catalog. She also has founded the Sara Blakely Foundation which is dedicated to helping women globally and locally through education and entrepreneurship.

One of the many unique facts about Blakely is that she has never taken a business course—instead, she 'follows her gut'. Her most important tip is this "Believe in your idea, trust your instincts, and don't be afraid to fail."

There is much to learn from Sara Blakely as you build your brand.

**Believe in yourself and your ideas** – If you do, you won't let anyone or anything stop you.

**Don't be afraid to fail** – There's much to learn from your failures, even more than you learn from your successes.

**Brands evolve** – Learn, grow, strive, improve. Branding is an ongoing process.

**Face your fears** – Replace your fear with faith. Take action. Blakely signed up for classes to face her fear of flying, but she was travelling so much, by plane of course, she never attended the class.

**Be persistent** – Every no gets you closer to the yes you seek as so eloquently stated in the book *Go For No* written by Richard Fenton and Andrea Waltz.

You never know where your big idea will come from—perhaps it will sneak up 'behind you' as it did with Sara Blakely. What's important is to know your personal brand. Embrace your why, identify what fulfills you, know your talents—and improve on them. That way, when your 'aha' moment comes along, you'll be in the best position possible to take advantage and achieve your dream results.

# Judge Judy Sheindlin

## From Dreamer to Judge—
## The Evolution of a Brand

If there were one word to describe life in the United States after World War II it may be 'boom'. There was an economic boom, a population boom and a boom in the television industry. As life returned to normal, most families could afford to own a TV and most of those sets tuned in to the Texaco Star Theater featuring Milton Berle. Viewers enjoyed his humor and the wide variety of entertainment. Some watched and dreamed of achieving fame as he had.

One such viewer was a young Jewish girl living in Brooklyn with her dentist father, her stay-at-home mother and her brother David. She had dreamed of being famous—of becoming a star—but let that dream slip when she determined that she didn't have the talent necessary. Instead she turned to education. She graduated high school in $3^{1}/_{2}$ years and was accepted into American University in Washington D.C. Upon graduating in 1963, she enrolled in that school's Washington School of Law—the only woman in a class of 126.

A year later she married and moved to New York City with her husband. In 1965, she earned her law degree and began to work as a corporate attorney at a cosmetics firm. She left after two years both because she wasn't fulfilled and to raise her two children. Five years later, a friend mentioned a job opening in the New York court system and she went for it and became a prosecutor in the family court system. There, she routinely prosecuted child abuse, domestic violence and juvenile offenders. The workload was not just enormous, it was difficult and emotionally draining.

She was known to be a very hard working, fair but no-nonsense litigator. Her home life wasn't as successful—she and her husband divorced after 12 years of marriage. Soon after, she met Jerry, the man who would become her second husband a year later. At home, hers was a family of seven—the couple, her two children and his three. At work, she continued to deal with families both dysfunctional and divided.

Mayor Ed Koch appointed her a family court judge. In that position she meted out her form of justice—swift, direct, effective and always no-nonsense. Four years later she was appointed supervising judge for the family court's Manhattan Division. Continued success and new positions didn't change her. She continued to be assertive, demanding, abrasive, firm, fair and sarcastic—but most of all she was effective. So much so that in 1993, the Los Angeles Times did a feature on her which led, in turn, to her being a featured segment on CBS' *60 Minutes*. With this newfound publicity, her persona and popularity continued to grow.

1996 was a landmark year for her. In February she published her first book, *Don't Pee on My Leg and Tell Me It's Raining*. That year—after twenty-five years and over 20,000 cases—she retired from family courts. She was approached with the concept of her presiding over real courtroom cases with real consequences—as a judge in a television courtroom. At the age of 54, she launched into a new career.

That show is now beginning its 20th season—its success being driven by the same assertive, sarcastic, fair and effective judge who first practiced in New York courts. Her show became the most watched syndicated show on television with audience numbers reaching 7 million viewers per week. After several nominations, she finally received an Emmy in 2013 for her work on the show. The little girl who quashed her thoughts of becoming a major television star is now earning $47 million *per year*. Milton Berle would have been both proud and jealous.

This success doesn't define a brand—rather, it's the result of Judith Sheindlin, Judge Judy, being a fearless brand.

## Fearless Brands remain true to themselves yet continue to evolve

Judy Sheindlin has spent a lifetime growing, learning and evolving, yet she is nothing if not authentic and genuine. Her passion—her why—hasn't changed over her nearly five decades of work in the legal arena. She is driven to dispense justice—fairly, swiftly and effectively. Her mission is to change lives—standing up for the underdog and the abused while meting out verdicts which hold the guilty accountable and urging them to change their ways.

Judge Judy has been tested, confronted and questioned by attorney's, defendants—even plaintiffs. Many assume her to be a cold-hearted woman. In her 1993 *60 Minutes* segment, an attorney who had just been quite forcefully admonished is seen clearly calling the judge a 'bitch'. Yet, Sheindlin has a warm, caring and loving side.

She and her husband Jerry, presided over each of their children's marriages (four of five are married). In 1990 she and Jerry divorced largely due to the impact Judy's father's death had on her. Within a year they had remarried. Sheindlin is a stereotypical doting grandmother.

Dare to cross her however, and you're certain to see how assertive a woman just five feet two inches tall can be. You're likely to hear any number of her trademark phrases which include "If you live to be a hundred, you will never be as smart as me. On your BEST day, you're not as smart as *I* am on my WORST day." and "...I eat morons like you for breakfast. You're gonna be crying before this is over." But then what would you expect from the woman who's second book is titled *Beauty* Fades, *Dumb is Forever*.

There are two key lessons from Judge Judy which anyone building their own brand must know

**Keep Evolving Your Brand** – A brand is not static—it is fluid. A brand changes with time—it must change to remain relevant and vital. Judy Sheindlin continued to evolve as a person—as a brand. Her why hasn't changed...but her what has. She has improved her skills and learned new ones while assuming new challenges and roles in her life. Throughout those evolutions, she has remained both authentic and relevant.

**It's Never Too Late** – Because brands are fluid, it's never too late to embark on a new journey. Sheindlin began her current career twenty years ago at the age of 54. If you believe that 'my ship has sailed' or that 'I'm just too old', then you really need to rethink your brand. Reevaluate your why. Re-ignite your passion. Refresh your skills—or learn new ones.

Judge Judy is a powerful firecracker in a small package. That's who she is. You just need to be you—the best you possible. You can always evolve your brand, strengthen your brand, become a fearless brand. Why should you? Simple—for the results—to achieve your dream results—just as an adult Judy Sheindlin realized the dreams of her youth.

# Queen Elizabeth II

## Branding Royalty—How Queen Elizabeth Stands the Test of Time

Little girls love to fantasize about becoming a princess, living a special life filled with attention and riches. In reality, very few actually have their dream become a reality. The fact is that most princesses are born into royalty. Such was the case with Elizabeth, born in London, England on April 21, 1926. Her father was Prince Albert, the second son of King George V, the reigning monarch of England, and his wife, Queen Mary.

As a child the girl, known as Lilibet, enjoyed all of the privilege of royalty. She lived the storybook life most girls imagine. When she was 10, however, things began to change. Her grandfather, King George died. As the eldest son, her uncle became King Edward VII. That would change quickly as well.

Edward was in love with an American woman and had to choose between the throne and his love. When Edward followed his heart, Lilibet's father ascended to the throne as King George VI.

World War II broke out in 1939. The 14 year old princess began making radio broadcasts directed at the children of England. Her message was calm and direct—"All will be good as God will protect us and bring us victory and peace." Towards the end of the war, she trained to become a driver and mechanic along-side other women. That was her first true experience with the "non-royal" world.

In 1947, she married Philip Mountbatten, a man she had first met when she was 13. The next year she gave birth to a son, Charles. A daughter, Anne, followed two years later. Her father, King George, died on February 6, 1952—Elizabeth succeeded to the throne. Westminster Abbey, the site of her marriage, also hosted her official coronation in June of 1953.

That began a reign which would see rapid change and turbulent times. England's position as a global power would diminish. England's role in the world and its economy would go through major transformation. Societal norms would change as would many people's perceptions about the role of England's royalty. Throughout it all, Queen Elizabeth acted with an unwavering devotion to duty and country. She displayed a sense of pragmatism, an example of which was initiating regular meetings with England's Prime Minister.

The British Empire had evolved to the Commonwealth of Nations. The Queen traveled the world in her role as head of the Commonwealth, including several significant visits. She visited Germany in 1965, the first monarch to do so in over fifty years. In 1976 she went to the United States for the bicentennial celebration of independence from British rule. Her trip to the Middle East in 1979 included visits to several countries including Saudi Arabia, Oman, and the United Arab Emirates, resulted in world-wide respect for the Queen and Britain.

The reign that began in 1952 continues to this day, making her the longest reigning monarch in British history. She celebrated her 90th birthday yesterday (April 20, 2016). There have been countless positives during Queen Elizabeth's reign. On the other hand, she has seen and dealt with family turbulence and scandal, political firestorms, worldwide financial crises and a rise in terrorism. Through it all, she is perhaps the most loved monarch ever. She remains a symbol of strength, resolve, reason and decorum.

Queen Elizabeth has accomplished so much for so long because she is a fearless brand. She is branding royalty.

## Fearless Brands are consistent in character

Queen Elizabeth is much beloved in England and throughout the world. She is the epitome of consistency. Her reign has provided much needed continuity during a century of volatility and change. Her devotion to duty, country, tradition and family has been unwavering.

The amount of money it takes to support the Queen and the royal family is questioned by some. What they don't take into account, however, is that Queen Elizabeth II is the embodiment of Britain's national identity. The goodwill, tourism and connections with the world that exist because of Queen Elizabeth are invaluable. Rarely, if ever, has a country benefited so much from the leadership and presence of a person who has no legal standing in the government of that country.

Very few will become a princess—much less a queen—yet there is much to learn from Queen Elizabeth II about building a brand.

**Be true to your purpose** – For nearly 65 years, Queen Elizabeth has held true to her sense of duty as a royal. She has maintained her primary focus on doing what is best for her country. She understands that doing so is her purpose as the Monarch of the Commonwealth. By so doing, she has accomplished much for England, and its people, that an elected official couldn't. Want to be a fearless brand? Know your purpose. Pursue it passionately with every skill you have.

**Remain relevant** – For someone who grew up with all the privilege of a royal, Elizabeth has consciously taken the 'non-royals' into consideration. She has made the monarchy more relevant through several actions. She dropped many formalities which no longer resonated. She increased accessibility to a variety of sites and treasures which were once restricted. She welcomed a much reduced level of government funding for the monarchy. Your brand has to be consistent—yet adjustments are essential to remain relevant.

**Keep your heart in your brand** – This quote from the Queen best sums up this point. "I cannot lead you into battle. I do not give you laws or administer justice but I can do something else—*I can give my heart and my devotion* to these old islands and to all the peoples of our brotherhood of nations.' Trust your heart. Bring the love.

Queen Elizabeth II is a magnificent woman. She is the consummate fearless brand. You and I will almost assuredly never become royalty. We can, however, become fearless brands. How? Learn from the Queen—know your purpose, remain relevant and put your heart into your brand.

# Malala Yousafzai

## Meet Malala—A Truly Fearless Advocate for Education

There are countless children who love school—who love to learn. Many are afforded that opportunity freely—with easy access to schools, highly motivated teachers and the latest text books. For others, there isn't that same access to education. Often times it is those children—the ones with keen desire to learn yet limited resources—who seem to truly cherish the learning opportunity they do have available, no matter how meager.

Such was the case with a young girl who lived in Mingora, Pakistan. She and her fellow students would study chemistry equations by chanting them, learning Urdu grammar, drawing 'maps' of the human blood circulation system and writing stories. She was fifteen in 2012 and out of concerns for her safety, her mother had her travel to school by rickshaw—she would return home by bus—a white Toyota van.

Taking precautions was more than justified as her city—in the middle of the Swat Valley—was a hot bed for the Taliban. One of their extremist beliefs was that girls should not go to school—should not pursue an education. Her father, himself an outspoken

opponent, had already seen a friend and fellow campaigner shot and killed by the Taliban.

On October 9th, 2012, she and several other girls, boarded the van which would take them home. This day, however, things would be different. The van was flagged down by a young Taliban man who asked for the girl by name. He had sought her, in particular, as she was very outspoken about her right to an education—for herself and all girls.

That afternoon in the Toyota, she was the only girl who was not covered—contrary to custom—and once she had been identified, the man held up a pistol and with his hand shaking, fired three shots. One hit her in the cheek just under her eye socket. Another, hit her shoulder, passing through and also hitting a second girl. The third bullet hit a third girl in the hand.

She was rushed to the intensive care unit of the Combined Military Hospital in Peshawar. Her cheek had shattered sending bone shards into her face and brain. The Doctor told her parents that she likely would lose some facial movement and that her looks were certain to be altered. This concerned her father, in particular, as he had always called his daughter 'my heavenly smile and laughter'.

She ultimately awoke after being transported to Birmingham in the U.K. It was then that she learned she was deaf in one ear and that her jaw didn't seem to move in a normal manner. Nerves in her face had been affected—she had lost the ability to smile. A month after she was shot, she underwent an operation that was hoped would help heal the damaged nerve. A cochlear implant had been inserted into her head to help her hearing. After several weeks, she regained some facial movement to the point that she could smile and wink.

Her parents' concern over the physical effect of the bullets was not something she shared—she was happy to be alive, to be able to speak, hear and continue to learn. She took a very active and dominant role in decisions concerning her care. The shooting failed to silence her—just as it had failed to kill her. Instead, it sparked an intense desire to fight harder and more vocally for the rights for girls to receive an education in her homeland. On her 16th birthday, July 12, 2013, she addressed a specially convened youth group at the United Nations in New York.

That speech, was broadcast around the world. She would go on to win the Nobel Peace Prize and write a book about her story. Her story is almost unbelievable and her accomplishments seemingly improbable—but they are not what makes the person a fearless brand. Malala Yousafzai—the author of the book *I Am Malala*—is fearless well beyond branding...as a matter of fact, she has never given a thought to herself as a brand.

## Fearless Brands focus on results—not their brand

Malala Yousafzai is a magnificent human being. In telling her story, it was important for me to realize—and accept—that she has no interest in building a brand, upgrading a brand or even thinking of herself as a brand. Very simply, hers is a story of commitment, dedication and true fearlessness.

From a very early age, she was instilled with the belief that education would be the key to her future. An education would allow her to pursue a professional career which would lead to the freedom to live as she chose. Her father was an educated man who had actually owned a school. The entire Swat Valley had been known as a bastion of learning beginning in the 1940's under the leadership of a line of Walis—rulers of the principality—who were committed to providing an education for all of their people. That changed in the early 2000's as the Taliban—with their extremist views—began to have a significant influence on the region.

Malala would unwittingly become the symbol of education rights. She continues to be a strong advocate for the right for girls to receive an education—in her home country of Pakistan and throughout the world. Along with her family, she now lives in Birmingham due to the ongoing threat of harm and death which exist in her home. When asked what the Taliban was likely thinking today—Malala said "I think they may be regretting that they shot Malala," she says. "Now she is heard in every corner of the world."

No, Malala has no interest in the concept of a personal brand—yet there is so much to learn from her when you work on yours.

**Embrace your vision completely** – Nothing, up to and including the threat of death, would deter Malala from her pursuit of an education. It is a belief which begins in her very core. As you work on your brand, make absolutely certain that you know—and embrace—your why.

**Make your vision bigger** – What began as a quest to receive an education just for herself, has exploded to a mission to create education opportunities for girls—and everyone—worldwide. Ask yourself this—"Is my why—my vision—big enough? Am I as fully committed as I can be? How can I increase the value I provide to the world?"

Work to make your brand have the greatest possible impact on those you are meant to serve. Make your vision bigger. Make your commitment stronger.

# Kirsten Green

## She's Bucking Boundaries and Building Brands

The University of California, Los Angeles (UCLA) boasts an enrollment of well over 40,000 students. It's not a challenge to find co-eds who are bright, energetic, attractive and talented. Kirsten easily fit that profile. She graduated in 1993 with a B.A. in Business Economics. She went to work at Deloitte & Touche where, having earned her C.P.A., she was a Senior Accountant. After three years she served a short stint as an analyst at Donaldson, Lufkin & Jenrette, an Investment Banking firm.

Her next move came in 1998 when she became a Vice-President at Bank of America Securities. There she was an equity research analyst—focusing on the specialty retail sector. Studying companies such as Abercrombie & Fitch, The Gap, Pottery Barn Urban Outfitters and other 'hot' retailers, afforded her keen insights and unique perspective on that category. Her experience broadened further when she was recruited to head an in-house team where she was the lead consumer-focused investment professional.

She realized that the specialty sector and the build out of malls represented what might be the last big cycle for retail. The turn of the century saw an overabundance of stores, driven in part by the explosion of online competition. With eBay and

Amazon leading the way, consumers began to embrace technology. Her experience, her education and her instincts told her that the retail landscape was going to change—drastically.

There was little doubt that technology would drive the next cycle of retail. The chance to become involved at the early stage of investments and be a part of the next iteration of retail intrigued her. She left her job and began to network, to learn, to seek experience. She formed Forerunner Ventures—based in San Francisco—in 2003.

She faced several barriers, each seemingly more insurmountable than the last. For starters, she was low-profile—she had not built a company, was not an operations expert and did not have the bluster and bravado typical of many investors and she certainly didn't have a technology background. Having a financial background was not common in the tech sector. What may have been her most daunting barrier is that she was—well... a she.

Fortunately, she was not one to let convention keep her from reaching her goals. By 2006 she had begun to make single investments in one-off partnerships in the $1–$1.5 million dollar range. She focused on investing in private companies learning and partnering as she went. Her criteria was different than most other investors. Rather than seeking to invest in the latest gimmick or quick flash idea—she sought seed stage companies whose founders had a connection with their products.

Her experience led her to look for companies with a solid value proposition—a company whose architecture could build a brand over time. Ideas and products which were relevant to consumers would achieve a high emotional ROI—or consumer loyalty. Her keen understanding of retail and consumer sales—which many assumed would be a negative—turned out to be one of her unique strengths and a key to success.

Today, Forerunner Ventures has invested in more than 30 companies with an investment portfolio of well over $100 million. Her first three major deals were Birchbox, Bonobos and Warby Parker—those companies now have a combined value of over $1 billion. Their list of company investments now includes Dollar Shave Club, Shuddle, Guildery and Chloe + Isabel to name but a few. This success is the result of the efforts of a fearless brand - Kirsten Green.

## Fearless Brands defy convention— undaunted by traditional barriers

Kirsten Green is anything but normal in the world of venture capitalists (VCs). She drives success by following her instincts, experience and values—in so doing, she has had significantly more wins than flops.

Green believes that consumers are in the driver's seat in this era of technology driven retail. She seeks companies that have a sound strategy of connecting with customers and knowing what resonates with them. Selling on value—vs price—is key in her assessments. Where does the product fit? Does the consumer want it—need it—will they pay for it?

Another key element of Green's—and Forerunner's—success is that she is committed to being a good partner with the entrepreneur's she invests in. She encourages and fosters connections between her portfolio companies which makes great sense given the complementary nature of many of their products.

It is estimated that females comprise barely 10% of the venture capital industry—that number declines at the partner level.

In spite of that, Kirsten Green—and her all female company—is making a mark in the investment world.

Unlike several of her female predecessors, Green is able to be completely transparent in her dual roles of VC partner and mother. Her business life and family life are aligned—by example, she has had staff meetings at her home while on maternity leave.

Kirsten Green is an amazing business person—who happens to be a female. There is a great deal to learn from her when it comes to building your brand and achieving dream results.

**Find your why** – As with most of us, Kirsten Green's key to success wasn't immediately clear—discovering her purpose required a variety of positions over an extended period. Explore a variety of roles, take chances, explore your options. Remember, discovering your why is rarely instantaneous, rather, it's a process—so be both patient and diligent.

**Build and deliver value** – As Green learned, value is not defined by price. Discover and clarify your value proposition. importantly, be certain that it is relevant—that it resonates with your target audience. When your brand fulfills your customers' wants and needs—you're delivering value.

**Seek to collaborate and empower** – It was Aristotle who said "The whole is greater than the sum of its parts." That statement speaks to the power of collaboration—the sharing of skills, perspective and support. It also encourages empowerment—leveraging inclusion and teamwork. Whether it's a team member, an employee or a trusted advisor, there is strength in numbers.

Kirsten Green has certainly differentiated herself from her 40,000 fellow UCLA students. She honed her skills, tapped into her passion and discovered how to add relevant value to the world. You can do the same—it's really that simple—it's just not easy.

# Robin Roberts

## "Go on With Your Bad Self!"

Tuskegee is a town of about 12,000 people in the southeastern portion of Alabama. It is home to Tuskegee University—a predominately black school founded in 1881—that developed a national reputation for academics and philanthropy under the leadership of its first director, Booker T. Washington. The town is also known as the home to one of the most famous air squadrons of World War II—the Tuskegee Airmen.

One of those pilots, Lawrence Roberts, returned home and married Lucimarian Tolliver—together they had four children. Their youngest—a girl—was born on November 23, 1960. She grew up, however, in a different small town—Pass Christian—on the Gulf Coast of Mississippi about 60 miles east of New Orleans. She attended Pass Christian High School where she stood out academically as well as in sports—notably basketball and tennis. She was a gifted player which resulted in her being offered a full scholarship to play basketball at Louisiana State University. While impressed with both its academics and its campus—she determined that it was just too large for her to feel comfortable.

Leaving Baton Rouge, a sign for Southeastern Louisiana University caught her attention. She decided to visit that school

and found her home. She received a scholarship—but to play tennis—which she did in addition to playing on the basketball team.
She was one of only three girls who had over 1,000 points (1,446)
and over 1,000 rebounds (1,034) while playing for the university.
She continued to excel scholastically, graduating cum laude with
a Bachelor of Arts degree in Communications.

Determined to follow in the footsteps of her older sister who
was a news anchor for a television station in New Orleans, her first
job was at WDAM TV in Hattiesburg, MS where her love of sports
and her passion for journalism landed her the dual responsibility
of dong sports reports and anchoring the news. It was 1983 and
for the next several years she continued to excel at broadcasting—
moving to ever larger markets—eventually landing a positions at
a television station and doing radio in Atlanta. Beginning in 1995,
she also contributed special reports for the ABC network's national morning show—"Good Morning America".

That led to her being hired by ESPN, "The Worldwide Leader in Sports"—which like ABC—is owned by the Walt Disney
Company. There she became the first black woman to anchor the
network's flagship program—Sports Center. The combination of
her tremendous sports experience, top-notch broadcasting talent
and her engaging personality made her a favorite with viewers,
athletes and the network. As is the case with many ESPN person-
alities, she developed several 'trademark' sayings—perhaps most
her most popular being 'Go on with your bad self'.

Her popularity grew and with it so did her career. In March
of 2005 she was named co-anchor of the ABC morning show—
which led to what—at least then—was her most emotional challenge at work. In August of that year, she had to cover the impact

of Hurricane Katrina. That storm caused catastrophic damage across the entire Gulf including her home of Pass Christian. Her high school was completely leveled—and through it all, her professionalism never wavered.

She went on to lead Good Morning America to capture the rating of number one morning show, was the first reporter to interview President Obama, traveled with First Lady Laura Bush to the Middle East, with former president Bill Clinton to Africa, has hosted prime time specials and ABC's Oscar pre-show. She has won a share of three Emmy's but perhaps the most telling honor she has earned is ESPN's Arthur Ashe Courage Award.

All of these accomplishments were achieved because Robin Roberts is a fearless brand.

## Fearless Brands live with courage

Robin Roberts' career is no doubt impressive—but to limit one's view to just her work life is to miss the essence of the woman. Her success has been driven by the value she consistently delivers to the public by embracing her passion and applying her tremendous skills. Roberts' true appeal—her real strength—is that she is genuine. She is a positive person who loves life, sports and people—and that comes through loud and clear.

Perhaps her most significant attribute is courage. She had the courage to realize that LSU was not right for her and followed her mind and heart. She had the courage to follow in her sister's journalistic footsteps—yet be true to herself. She had the courage to allow the stories to be the focus while letting her personality shine through. She possessed a courage that most weren't familiar with....but that would change.

In 2007, Roberts was diagnosed with breast cancer. While that, sadly, is not unusual—the manner in which she went about dealing with it is. She showed the courage to share her diagnosis—but also shared her efforts to fight her condition. She won—she beat cancer—and went back to *Good Morning America* and a supportive and grateful audience.

Her breast cancer treatment did what was intended—an unintentional consequence was discovered in 2011 when Roberts was diagnosed with myelodysplastic syndrome (MSD)—a very rare blood disorder. Again she chose to share her challenges with the public—not to elicit pity—but to build awareness of the disease and the critical role bone marrow could play in a cure for MSD and many other diseases. Her efforts, as well as those of her colleagues at ABC, resulted in an 1,800% increase in registrations at Be The Match which has and will save hundreds of lives.

When she again returned to *Good Morning America*—in 2013—the show achieved its highest ever viewership when an estimated 6.1 million people tuned in. Roberts courage, gratitude and positivity were all communicated in her spectacular smile—and tears of joy. Her appreciation for life—her happiness—and her peace in life allowed her to once again demonstrate her courage as a person.

In 2014 she publicly announced that she was gay and has been in a long-term committed relationship. Courage and class allowed her to respond to her critics in a *Good Housekeeping* interview by saying simply—"...You don't go through a year like I did to not be happy and not make your own choices."

As you continue to upgrade your brand—it's perhaps best to focus on three of Robin Robert's quotes:

"Life is not so much what you accomplish as what you overcome."

"I'm no Pollyanna, but I believe optimism is a choice—a muscle that gets stronger with use."

"Right foot, left foot...just keep moving."

Embrace your passion, build on your talents and add relevant value to the world...become a fearless brand—or as Robin Roberts would say "Go on with your bad self!"

# Carmen Castillo

## Language, Gender nor a Hurricane
## Could Stop This Fearless Brand

She was born on the Spanish island of Mallorca—the sixth of ten children. She first stood out because of her natural blonde hair—her family warmly referring to her as the 'blonde sheep' of the family. The fact that her family was quite poor did not diminish her rich imagination. From a very early age she dreamed of life outside of Spain. She would study foreign languages, imagining what life would be like in those countries.

She became smitten with the U.S when in 1987 she visited friends in Florida. She determined that it was time to follow her dream and moved to America where she enrolled in culinary school in Palm Beach. Having been trained as a chef, she headed to Buffalo, New York to visit friends. Once there, she spent months helping one of those friends—a woman who was both pregnant and battling cancer. That friend connected her with a new restaurant owner in need of a chef—a role she readily accepted.

One day a customer asked to meet the chef to pass on his praise for the food—a man who would have a significant impact on her future. That customer was the Chairman of the Superior Group, a national workforce solutions company based in

Western New York and a regular at the restaurant. Impressed with her drive and sales acumen, he took on the role of mentor as the two forged what would become a long-term relationship. With his guidance and mentoring, she developed plans to launch a business in South Florida.

On August 24, 1992, she went to her new office for the first time. It was that day that Hurricane Andrew hit Ft. Lauderdale, Florida. Having one's office devastated by a hurricane on the first day would deter most people—but not this transplanted Spaniard. She wasn't about to walk away—rather, she started to build her business knocking on door after door. Her company, Superior Design International Inc. (SDI) offered Managed Services Programs and Independent Contractor Compliance Programs.

Her big break came when IBM engaged SDI for a major initiative in South Florida. The success of that project led to SDI being added to the vendor selection process, opening the door for further opportunities with larger clients. Business began to skyrocket. She was determined to build a global business and adopted a philosophy of "Build Globally, but Think Locally".

Currently SDI has business operations in the U.S., Argentina, Belgium, Canada, China, India, Slovakia, and the United Kingdom. They employ well over 2,000 people and have revenue in excess of $1.3 billion. Clients include, IBM, Office Depot, Motorola, Dell and Lenovo to name but a few. It is said to be the largest Latina-owned business in the country. The company's success is obvious but not what makes a fearless brand. This company was built by a fearless brand—Carmen Castillo—whose vision, passion, talent and drive made SDI what it is today.

## Fearless Brands are the heart and soul of the companies they build

Carmen Castillo is the epitome of a fearless brand—and also the American dream. She embraced her vision at an early age. She studied and refined her talents. She was not going to be easily derailed—actually she wouldn't be derailed period. Importantly, she understands that a successful CEO needs to be a visionary—anticipating new technology and trends and capitalizing on them before your competition. Castillo also believes that the head of a company needs to be the head of sales.

SDI holds multiple diversity certifications—woman owned, minority owned. Castillo believes in taking advantage of that status in order to help create a more even playing field. However, she is determined that SDI will be a corporation which is known for quality services and customer satisfaction that happens to be minority owned. Her company, like herself, will be successful based on its merit.

Carmen Castillo is an avid supporter of business diversity. She does so by proactively seeking qualified diversity businesses to fill SDI's needs whenever possible. She also provides mentoring to those companies—continuing the practice of her own mentor from her days as a chef. That relationship remains active to this day—each benefiting from the other's wisdom, insights and knowledge.

As with each Friday's Fearless Brand—there's much to learn about building your own brand when looking at Carmen Castillo.

**Embrace your dreams** – Perhaps the single greatest aspect of every fearless brand is that they discover—and embrace—their why. They are driven to achieve their vision—remaining focused on that rather than the material gains.

**Remain teachable** – Castillo recognizes the power and value of having a mentor—or mentors. There's nothing better than receiving the wisdom, insights and perspective of someone who's 'been there, done that'—especially when they have a genuine interest in you and your vision.

**Pass it on** – Being a mentor can be even more beneficial than having a mentor. Passing on your guidance and best thinking certainly helps those on the receiving end—but the satisfaction you get from helping others is a benefit by itself.

You needn't survive a hurricane in order to become a fearless brand as Carmen did. However, there will always be challenges, road blocks and deterrents on the way to building your brand. The key is how you handle those challenges. Stay in touch with your why, be open to learning, help others and you will be successful and achieve dream results.

# Indra Nooyi

## To Her It's a Calling—Not a Career

In October of 1955, a banker and his wife welcomed their baby girl into the world in Madras (now Chennai) southern India. At that time it was generally accepted that a girl would follow a certain path to marriage and motherhood. This mother saw things differently, however, telling the girl 'I want to get you married when you are 18, and make sure you aspire to be the prime minister.' The mother developed games based on world problems and had the children develop solutions. Having a keen focus on school grades was common to their culture and the girl excelled. Her grandfather, a district judge, was also a big influence in her life. It was he that believed his granddaughters could be whatever they chose to be—even in a society which was very gender driven. She embraced that philosophy and began to play cricket—not watch—play. She showed even more conviction to follow her interests regardless of expectation when she became the lead singer and guitarist in an all-girl rock band. She continued to pursue excellence in school and earned a bachelor's degree in 1976 having majored in chemistry and followed that with an MBA degree two years later.

She became a product manager at a textile firm but quickly moved and held the same position for Johnson & Johnson. There, she was given the challenge of launching Stayfree sanitary napkins in India—a task made even tougher as that product could not be legally advertised. She succeeded by going direct to the consumer in a variety of ways. After two years she applied to Yale University without any real expectations—but she was accepted and offered financial aid. In spite of extreme societal pressure—this path would make her unmarriageable—her parents fully supported her plans.

At Yale, she thrived—enthusiastically embracing management concepts which, to her, were unique. She was eager to learn—even partaking in a survival expedition to the Arctic as part of the team building ideas being taught. Her interest in 'bat and ball' sports led her to learn baseball and become a fan of the Yankees. She learned the sport but also the lingo often used in business—e.g. hit a home run. She followed the Chicago Bulls to learn about leadership. Through it all she held dearly to her Indian heritage—her identity.

Successful stints at the Boston Consulting Group and Motorola led to her becoming a Senior VP of Strategy at Asea Brown Boveri—a company she later described as a $6 billion startup. She had become known in the corporate world and was highly sought after for top management positions in a variety of companies. PepsiCo brought in a former CEO who had been raised in India to help persuade her to join their company. It worked. She joined Pepsi in 1994 as the senior VP of corporate strategy and development.

Her experience, education and management skills led her to drive some mega deals. She orchestrated the spinoff of Taco Bell, KFC and Pizza Hut. She drove the acquisition of Tropicana and Quaker Oats. She was named CEO in 2006. The following year she added chairman of the board of directors to her resume. PepsiCo thrived. She has been named to numerous lists compiled by respected organizations such as the *Wall Street Journal, Fortune* and *Time*—most recently being named the third Most Powerful Women in business on Fortune's 2014 list. To the surprise of some, she has also been married for thirty-four years and raised two highly educated and motivated daughters.

Her amazing list of accomplishments is not what defines her brand—rather she achieved so much because Indra Nooyi is a fearless brand.

## Fearless Brands don't seek a job— they follow their calling.

Nooyi has shattered most stereotypes, crashed through barriers and dismissed the societal concerns which existed in her native culture. Throughout her career she has remained authentic—true to her heritage, committed to her personal interests and driven to achieve large-scale success for her company. Pepsico had a a strong interest and need to diversify by gender and ethnicity. Hiring Indra Nooyi did that—and more.

Nooyi has never shied away from her ethnicity—her being Indian. She has summarily dismissed reports that she wears a sari to the boardroom—or even to work for that matter. She not only believes that doing so would be distracting but that she has an obligation to fit in with the norm—quoting the old saying that 'when in Rome....'

One question she is often asked is—"Can women 'have it all'?" According to Nooyi, being a CEO has to be a calling—that it's not a career. It requires you to be 'all in', to love what you're doing, to be totally consumed. It is her passion to make Pepsi bigger and stronger than it was. She has to determine at any given moment if she is going to be an executive, a mother or a wife.

There has to be somewhat of a balance—but being a successful CEO takes a lot of time, focus and effort.

Indra Nooyi is a nearly perfect example of a fearless brand as evidence by these four factors:

**Authenticity** – Nooyi remains a woman proud to be Indian; continues to love her music, singing often; loves sports, especially cricket and wears her native dress when appropriate. Yet she has been able to integrate her heritage into her current profession, geography and culture.

**Passion** – She loves what she does—as she says, it's a calling. That passion allows her to give her all to Pepsi—to her professional pursuits.

**Skills and education** – From early childhood she has been a voracious learner. Nooyi has embraced her talents yet done whatever was necessary to continue learning—expanding and improving her talents.

**Relevance** – What's the result of this combination of passion and skill? Powerful and relevant leadership and strategy—and a highly successful company.

It's not necessary that you join a band or follow sports to successfully build your fearless brand. What is required is to be authentic—find what motivates you, sharpen your skills, be relevant, simply put—matter. Matter to yourself and matter to those you serve. Make sure you find your calling.

# Anne Mulcahy

## You Brand Like a Girl!

Born in Rockville Centre, NY in 1952 she was the only daughter in a family with four sons. That could have been daunting for her had it not been for her parents. They encouraged her to compete equally with her brothers and that's exactly what she did. In so doing, she learned how to hold her own in the face of adversity and criticism. She learned the power of listening in order to understand people and situations. These were lessons which would stay with her throughout her life.

She went on to earn a degree in English and Journalism from Marymount College of Fordham University and then began a career in field sales with Xerox. She married—a sales manager with Xerox—and had two children, both sons. At times during her sixteen years in sales she entertained thoughts of leaving her career to spend more time with her boys but she did not. She rose through the ranks—at a rather brisk pace.

She was named VP of human resources in 1992. In three years she became VP and staff officer of worldwide customer operations. From there Senior VP and chief staff officer. By the end of the century, she was named president of general market operations and COO. The lessons from her early years played a major role in her success. She listened to customers—and employees—and she made the necessary tough decisions. However, the real challenges were still to come.

Ten years after leaving field sales she was named the first ever female CEO of Xerox. The company was in dire straits. Expenses were too high, profit margins too low. With $18 billion in debt many were advocating—or at least expecting—Xerox to declare bankruptcy. As if that weren't enough, the company's billing and accounting practices were the subject of an extensive investigation by the Securities and Exchange Commission (SEC).

She began by saying the Xerox business model was unsustainable but that bankruptcy was not an option. Her goal was to re-establish Xerox as a great company. She met with 100 top executives and asked for their full commitment—98 did so. Next she went back to her corporate roots—to the field to meet with customers—to listen. When one customer said she should 'kill the Xerox culture' she responded—'I am the Xerox culture'. She was deeply committed to Xerox and its resurrection.

Making the tough decisions—she sold off some of Fuji Xerox, eliminated 28,000 employees and cut billions in expenses. A settlement was reached with the SEC. She stood her ground, however, when it came to Research and Development, refusing to cut back on R&D. Her vision for the future relied on technology and transitioning to a digital content management company—a service based company.

Her efforts paid off. Under her leadership, Xerox saw full year profitability in 2002. She cut most of the fat—without losing muscle. What began to emerge was a newly vibrant company with restored integrity, improved financial performance, a more solid management structure and importantly, a keen focus on the customer. She was the first woman ever to be named CEO of the year by *Chief Executive Management* magazine. These accomplishments are not what defines a fearless brand. Rather, they were achieved because the CEO, Anne Mulcahy, is herself, a fearless brand.

## Fearless Brands combine listening and courage to create conviction

Anne Mulcahy transitioned Xerox from a crippled company to one that was positioned for current—and future—success. She was not a financial expert—she actually spent endless hours with experts to learn the essentials. To achieve such a turnaround Mulcahy relied on her core strengths—listening and standing her ground. She was focused and decisive—making tough decisions with a vision for the future.

Xerox is significantly better off because of Anne Mulcahy's leadership. She was CEO for ten years, stepping down at the age of 57. That marked the end of an era, but not the end of a fearless brand.

While at Xerox and after retiring, Mulcahy has served on several public boards including Citicorp and Johnson & Johnson. Importantly, she is bringing her strengths—courage, listening, conviction—to the non-profit world. Since 2010, she has been Chairman of the Board of Trustees of Save The Children Federation, Inc., an organization dedicated to creating lasting change in the lives of children throughout the world.

Being an advocate for women is both a responsibility and an opportunity that Mulcahy embraces. She acknowledges relative parity at the entry level yet is keenly aware that such equality does not exist at the executive level—in business and in government. As a role model, mentor, and advocate, she is a force that will have an impact.

There is a great deal to learn from Anne Mulcahy when it comes to building a fearless brand.

**Compete on an equal basis** – Be fair, be confident, be empathetic and be determined.

**Listen** – Listening is the key to better understanding others—and ourselves. Listen with intent.

**Have ambition ... and humility** – A healthy dose of ambition is critical to success—have bold aspirations. However, blindly charging ahead can be disastrous. Know—and embrace—both your strengths and your shortcomings.

**Accept reality but have the courage to change** – Anne Mulcahy's words say it best. "Do not defend yourself against the inevitable. Companies disappear because they can't reinvent themselves."

When it comes to understanding the meaning of branding for results—you need look no further than Anne Mulcahy. She began building her fearless brand at a very young age. She received tremendous advice and support from her parents. Today, she continues to refine and polish her brand. The results are powerful.

Use Anne Mulcahy as a role model when building your own fearless brand and when someone says "You brand like a girl!"— say "Yes I do. Thank you!"

# Dondi Scumaci

## Ready, Set...Grow!—Your Value

She was born in Oregon, into a family of ranchers and farmers. Her parents had moved to the city to raise her, believing they were providing her with opportunities they had lacked having grown up on farms. Ironically, her desire was to live on a ranch. As a young girl she wanted two things—to be a writer and to own a horse. In the city, her bicycle was her horse.

Her grandfather came to live with the family—a living arrangement not all that uncommon. Unique was that he was totally sightless, having been blinded in a mining accident as a young man, although being without sight did not keep him from achieving his life vision. He had built a very successful ranching and farming enterprise and partook in the many gifts life presented.

She became his eyes, taking after dinner walks through the neighborhood, taking him to the store to buy supplies to tie fishing flies, guiding him wherever they decided to go. They became fast friends and their shared experiences would come to play a major role in her life.

In that era, girls were expected to get married, have a baby and perhaps find a nice banking job. She did all three. That marriage played out badly but she was a star in the banking world.

She delivered exceptional results and become the youngest female vice-president in that Seattle bank. As a result, she was recruited to a national position in Minnesota

A factor in her success was having a boss who was self-confident enough to empower, encourage and mentor her – but with the move came a new boss. This one was not the open, supportive, collaborative mentor her previous boss had been. Things went badly—so much so that she ultimately decided to take a huge leap and start her own business.

All her experiences combined to get her to the point of making this move—one filled with uncertainty, challenge and fear. What she realized, however, was that this move was her calling—it would allow her to fulfill her purpose. It was the opportunity she had been groomed for through all her experiences—both terrific and horrible. Today she is an internationally recognized and sought after consultant—the author of several best-selling books—and the owner of a horse which she keeps on her ranch in Texas.

These accomplishments are not what made her brand—they have been achieved because Dondi Scumaci has built herself into a fearless brand.

## Fearless Brands don't just discover their purpose—they actively develop, enhance and follow their calling.

Dondi began her business by focusing on the lessons and results she had learned by building relationships both within the bank and with their customers. She had come to recognize the power of having a mentor. It was this foundation that launched her success as a speaker, author and advisor. Dondi found that her message was desperately needed in corporate America—and that's where she put her efforts.

At one point, she asked her audience to think of a time in their personal life that they had benefitted from being mentored. To her surprise she had an 'aha' moment as her thoughts turned to the time she spent with her grandfather. She suddenly became more aware than ever that being his 'eyes' had taught her critical life lessons and honed three of her key attributes.

**Vision** – By guiding her 'Pop' she learned to look ahead—to see what was out front—to anticipate.

**Communication** – Effectively leading another person required very clear and effective communication.

**Balance** – When being leaned on—literally or figuratively—you must keep yourself steady and maintain your own balance.

Those traits allow her to be herself, to embrace her purpose and share these lessons in a powerful manner. Being vulnerable—being ok with showing her imperfections—has allowed Dondi's audiences, readers and mentees to relate with her on an unquestionably honest and intimate level. Allowing others to see that she embraces her flaws and shortcomings and in no way pretends to be perfect—provides the ultimate bond with those in contact with her. In her book *Ready, Set...Grow!* Dondi opens herself to the reader in a manner most are too fearful to. The day that she finished that book, it rained in Austin, ending a drought and with the rain came her tears as she rejoiced in the freedom writing that book brought to her.

Dondi learned that life and her actions should not be about herself—rather the focus should be outward. She discovered much greater and more effective results by looking out for other's interests first and addressing those opportunities. That approach allowed her to stay in touch with her calling—to meet her purpose in life. It should come as no surprise that Dondi's key mentor is Bob Burg—the force behind the book *The Go-Giver*.

One of her most powerful and oft-borrowed quotes is "Compliance will never take you where commitment can go."—her point being to nurture, mentor, encourage and support people so that they become committed. Companies who rely on forced compliance will never realize the same results or level of loyalty as those who create commitment.

Some of Dondi's lessons relate directly to branding. Here are but a few of her insights—which, if followed, will help you build your own fearless brand and enjoy the gifts of doing so.

**You have a purpose** – "We are all born with a purpose but I believe they don't come with batteries." says Dondi. It is not enough to know that you have a purpose—there is 'some assembly required'. Do the work, whatever it takes, to have your purpose blossom.

**Embrace your experiences—both good and bad** – Dondi's experiences helped her growth and understanding of other people. Your experiences make you who you are and lead directly to the next key point.

**You have value** – Dondi will also tell you that sometimes life will spindle, staple and mutilate but *your value* remains intact. Trust that you are never too small or insignificant—you offer unique perspective and have unique gifts.

**Ask the best questions** – The best way to facilitate success is to ask the best questions. As a result, not only do you get the best answers but you elevate the value of those being asked.

**Mentoring is powerful** – It is very simple—If you don't have a mentor, get one. If you are not a mentor, become one.

Dondi Scumaci is one of the most genuine, authentic, kind, caring and talented persons I have ever had the privilege to meet. Meeting her is one of the countless gifts I have received as a result of my involvement with The Go-Giver. Read her books and blogs. Follow her on social media. She is currently 'mentoring' her horse Fortunato and teaching him how to become a fearless brand. She is imminently qualified to do so because she herself is the embodiment of a fearless brand and proof that fearless brands can be—and are—built.

# Betty White

## Building Fearless Brands Creates Golden Results

She attended grade school at the Horace Mann School in Beverly Hills where she aspired to be a writer. With that in mind, she wrote the eighth grade graduation play and ended up starring in the lead role. It was then that she discovered her keen interest in performing and becoming an actress became her focus. She graduated from Beverly Hills High School in 1939 and began visiting Hollywood studios looking for work as an actress.

While no doubt disappointed, she was not deterred when she was told time and again that she was not photogenic enough. She turned to radio where she was a writer, the voice of various characters and read commercials. She broke into television by singing on a station in Los Angeles. Her continued pursuit of acting finally landed her first professional role at a community theater. Just as her career began to gain some momentum, World War II broke out—she did her part for the war effort as a volunteer.

At the same time, she continued to be active on radio—appearing on a variety of shows. By the end of the decade she had her own radio show. In 1949, she became co-host of a television variety show called *Hollywood on Television*. The next year, the girl who was not photogenic enough, was nominated for an

Emmy as Best Actress on television. She became the solo host of that show and the same year started a production company along with two men—a writer and a producer. Using the variety show as inspiration, they created—and she was the lead character—in a sitcom which became nationally syndicated. It was highly unusual at that time for a woman to have total control of creative on a TV show—both in front of and behind the camera. Imagine, a successful show co-produced and owned by a twenty-eight-year-old woman who still lived with her parents—in the 1950's.

She finally made her 'big screen' movie debut in 1962, where her role as a U.S. Senator was well received. She also pursued a position as a television game show host—a genre coming into its own at that time. Rather than being discouraged when told that the public wasn't ready for a female hostess, she shifted her focus to becoming a celebrity participant on a variety of game shows.

That exposure, coupled with being the voice of the Rose Bowl Parade for over a decade, resulted in growing fame, as well as a strong bond with audiences. In 1973, she landed a supporting actress role on a sitcom, playing the role of Sue-Ann Nivens. Her performance resulted in winning two of her three Emmy nominations for Outstanding Supporting Actress.

She had created a nearly thirty year career as an entertainer, comedienne and actress which would have fulfilled the dreams of countless women—and men. Yet this woman who was not photogenic enough for film, was the wrong gender to host a game show and the twenty-eight year old who had to create her own production company to pursue her dreams had barely scratched the surface.

After four *more* decades, her accomplishments and credits boggle the mind. On television alone she's done sitcoms, game shows, movies, variety shows and more. She's done countless commercials and authored seven books. Seven Emmy wins—including one, ironically, for Best Game Show Host. Multiple lifetime achievement awards—including one *twenty-five* years ago. There are just too many appearances and awards to list. None of this makes her a fearless brand. This incredible body of work—these amazing accomplishments—are because Betty White built a fearless brand.

## Fearless brands are resilient, positive and tenacious.

Betty White can be summed up in two words—America's Sweetheart. She's 92 now and is showing no signs of letting up—saying she has to keep working in order to continue her many efforts in support of animal rights. Given the length, variety and success of her career, it's hard to pick one role or accomplishment for which she is best known. Many will say The Golden Girls—others The Mary Tyler Moore Show. Millennials may know her best from the show *Hot In Cleveland*, *Betty White's Off Their Rockers* or even *Betty White Goes Wild!*.

She was featured in a Snickers commercial which debuted in the 2010 Super Bowl. That appearance sparked a social media campaign to have Betty White host *Saturday Night Live* which she did in May of that year, becoming the oldest person to ever host the show. Her episode generated the show's biggest ratings in eighteen months and earned Betty her seventh Emmy.

In addition to the happiness and laughs Betty White delivers—there is much to learn from her about building your fearless brand.

**Be resilient** – Throughout her career, White would not get discouraged at the many roadblocks in her path. Not photogenic enough? Fine, I'll work in radio—for now. A woman cannot host a game show? Well, I'll become one of the most popular celebrity participants—for now. Rather than allowing herself to get derailed, she kept an eye on her goal but focused on what she could do in the present that would allow her to reach her goal over time. Stay on the path to your goals—even though it will always include unexpected twists.

**Be positive** – White says that she's always positive—and that was the reason Bea Arthur of The Golden Girls didn't care for her. Her positive attitude allowed her to focus on the possibilities of every situation rather than getting derailed. Look for the opportunities that exist regardless of setbacks and disappointments—they always exist.

**Be tenacious** – Don't give up on your hopes and dreams—even if you're 92.

When asked what in Hollywood has she not yet done that she'd like to, she responded "Robert Redford". Certainly that's a funny line—but it also shows that she has realized virtually all of her goals. I submit that it's because she built a fearless brand that she's realized such incredible results. Embrace your passions and drive—recognize and continuously improve your skills—be relevant and you too can achieve stratospheric success. That's the magic of building your fearless brand.

# Epilogue

## Fearless Brands

$M$y book, *Women Who Won,* was born out of my weekly blog series—*Friday's Fearless Brand.*

I've spent most of my professional life working in the field of branding and the terms 'brand' and 'branding' are often misunderstood or overused. Helping clients and companies understand the true essence of successful branding led me to identify those brands—big and small—that best demonstrate what good branding is. In fact, I began to search out brands that were not only good, but were truly fearless.

What is a fearless brand? The answer needs to be broken down into two parts.

## What is a brand?
A brand can be a person, place or thing—it can be a business, a product or a service. Virtually everything is a brand, and very simply is the value that we perceive we will receive from a person, business or product.

The perception we have when we see a sign for Walmart is different to the perception we have when we see a sign for Target. The brand is not the sign or the store. The name, signs, ads and other communications are brand messaging. It's our thoughts and perceptions that define those brands for us.

The same principle holds true for people. We also define personal brands.

While we define a brand, a brand's value is built, managed and communicated to us. That's called brand management.

## What makes a brand fearless?

Simply put, a fearless brand is one which has achieved clarity as to its value and purpose. A fearless brand has attained the conviction that comes from true humility. Fearless brands accept their strengths and shortcomings exactly as they are—without deflection and without exaggeration.

Fearless, in this context, doesn't mean a lack of fear. Quite the contrary. Fear is real. Everyone has fears. What makes a brand fearless is honest self-awareness and self-knowledge. That conviction eliminates the fear of misrepresenting one's value. There is no fear of being discovered to be 'less than' or inadequate. Being fearless is the result of finding humility.

Authenticity is absolutely essential when building a fearless brand. Failure to be totally genuine will, eventually, degrade a brand's value, often in the blink of an eye. Being authentic drives consistency. Consistency drives trust. Trust is the heart of a fearless brand.

## There are three aspects to creating a fearless brand

**Passion** – Discovering and embracing one's passion. Simon Sinek refers to it as finding your 'why'. Others have referred to it as your motivation, your drivers, or your purpose. It's the intangible energy that creates your 'want to'.

**Talent** – Assessing one's skills and assets. What attributes enable you to do the things that motivate you? If your capabilities fall short, can they be improved through education, experience, or practice?

**Relevance** – Identifying the people and businesses that find relevance in your offering. The combination of your motivation and talents—your value proposition—has to pass the 'so what' test. Relevance must first be present for yourself—otherwise you'll not have true passion. If others don't find your offering relevant—your value is non-existent.

I've created this simple equation to define a fearless brand.

(passion + talent) x relevance = a fearless brand

Fearless branding is actually that simple—simple but not easy.

Building a fearless brand is an essential component to achieving success—as we define it. As evidenced by the amazing women in this book, and countless others, there are always challenges—some expected, others a complete surprise. Fearless brands have the self-awareness and self-assurance that they have what it takes to achieve their goals—regardless of the difficulty.

*Women Who Won* is a tribute to twenty-eight women—all who followed different paths, faced different challenges, and were driven by different passions—who are all truly fearless brands.

# Acknowledgements

Women Who Won is the result of the wide-ranging support, encouragement, counsel, advice, editing, friendship received from a collection of very special people in my life. My wife, Tara, whose encouragement, cheerleading, editing, and fandom started me—and keeps me—on this path. My friend Doug Wagner for his comment at the very beginning of my Friday's Fearless Brand blog series. Friend, mentor, and true gentleman Bob Burg, whose tireless support and endless belief in me is priceless. John David Mann, who provided encouragement, shared his writing expertise, and the gift of no-punches-pulled critiques delivered honestly yet lovingly. Cathy and Jack Davis, of Davis Creative, for their guidance, professionalism and patience.

# About the Author

## Bill Ellis

BILL ELLIS is a master at unlocking the fearless potential in others. A veteran of corporate brand management for more than 25 years at global beverage giant Anheuser-Busch, Bill has come to learn and deliver his true value in the past decade as a public speaker, certified coach and owner of a consultancy for personal and small business branding.

His weekly blog, **Friday's Fearless Brand**, has earned a following around the world as he masterfully highlights core elements of brands—whether people, places or organizations—that he considers to be fearless.

It is Friday's Fearless Brand that is the foundation for **Women Who Won**, a book sparked by Bill's twin granddaughters and his wish for their happy future as successful intrepid women. It is his hope that this compilation of stories of amazing women from all walks of life will inspire and remind—both men and women—that we all can win.

A devoted father, grandfather and husband, Bill divides his time between St. Louis, Missouri and Dubai, United Arab Emirates—travelling the world and broadening his knowledge and following along the way.

www.womenwhowon.com
www.brandingforresults.com

Made in the USA
Columbia, SC
06 September 2019